The 100 Most Asked Questions about God and the Bible

The 100 Most Asked Questions about God and the Bible

A Divine Guide to Answering Life's Hardest Questions for Yourself and Others with Wisdom, Compassion, and Confidence

Home Sweet Home Publishing

The original purchaser of this book has permission to reproduce the pages of this book for personal use only. No other parts of this publication may be reproduced in whole or in part, shared with others, stored in a retrieval system, digitized, or transmitted in any form without written permission from the publisher.

Copyright 2025, Home Sweet Home Publishing (Aria Capri International Inc). All rights reserved.

Authors:
Home Sweet Home Publishing

First Printing: April 2025

ISBN 978-1-998729-40-1 (Electronic book)

ISBN 978-1-998729-39-5 (Hardcover book)

ISBN 978-1-998729-38-8 (Paperback)

Dear Reader,

As the author of this book, thank you for walking this journey of faith and discovery.

If this book helped you find clarity, deepen your understanding, or start meaningful conversations about God and the Bible, I'd be truly grateful if you'd take a moment to share a quick review.

Just scan the QR code to leave your thoughts.

Your review encourages me and helps more parents, mentors, and everyday believers discover this resource and grow in their walk with God.

Thank you for being part of this mission to make biblical truth more accessible, one question at a time.

All the best in Christ,

Home Sweet Home Publishing

Want to Go Deeper? Get Your Free Bonus!

We've created a special companion resource just for you:

Start the Conversation – *25 Faith-Building Questions for Parents, Mentors, and Youth Leaders to Explore with Kids and Teens*

This free downloadable guide will help you turn the insights from this book into powerful, Christ-centered conversations with the next generation.

Claim your free copy by scanning the following QR code:

Whether you're a parent, mentor, or ministry leader, this tool will help you guide others with confidence, clarity, and grace.

Table of Contents

Introduction 8
How to Use This Book 9
Section 1: Understanding God 10
Section 2: Jesus Christ 17
Section 3: The Holy Spirit 24
Section 4: Sin and the Human Condition 33
Section 5: The Bible and Its Authority 42
Section 6: Christian Living and Ethics 51
Section 7: Church and Community 61
Section 8: Heaven and Hell 66
Section 9: End Times and Prophecy 75
Section 10: Faith in the Real World 85
Conclusion 96

Introduction

Questions about God and faith arise in every human heart. Some emerge during quiet moments of reflection, while others surface amid life's trials and joys. *Is God real? How can I know I'm saved? Why does suffering exist? Can the Bible be trusted in today's world?* These aren't merely intellectual puzzles—they're heartfelt inquiries that shape our understanding, guide our decisions, and influence our eternal destiny.

This book was created to walk alongside you through these questions.

Why This Book Matters

The purpose of this book is straightforward yet profound: to provide clear, biblically faithful answers to the most asked questions about God, faith, and the Christian life. These aren't speculative responses or personal opinions, but answers anchored in Scripture, delivered with pastoral sensitivity, and designed to strengthen your understanding and relationship with God.

Faith and questions aren't enemies. Honest questions often lead to deeper faith when approached with humility and guided by God's Word. The Bible contains many questions—from Abraham's "Will not the Judge of all the earth do right?" to the disciples' "Lord, are you at this time going to restore the kingdom to Israel?" God welcomes our sincere inquiries because they open the door to greater truth and intimacy with Him.

Who This Book Is For

This resource speaks to people at every stage of their spiritual journey:

- For the seeker wondering if Christianity makes sense, these pages offer thoughtful explanations without pressuring or judging.
- For the new believer navigating unfamiliar terrain, you'll find accessible answers to foundational questions about salvation, prayer, and Christian living.
- For the seasoned Christian encountering doubts or complex topics, these responses provide biblical clarity and renewed confidence.
- For parents or mentors helping others understand faith, this book equips you with concise, accurate explanations you can share with those you guide.

You don't need theological training to benefit from these pages. The language is straightforward without oversimplifying complex topics. Each answer aims to inform your mind and nurture your heart and strengthen your walk with Christ.

Where These Questions and Responses Come From

The questions explored in this book did not arise from abstract theological debates or isolated academic study; instead, they come from actual conversations with people wrestling with faith, doubt, and the complexities of life. These questions were drawn from pastoral counselling sessions, online forums, small group discussions, and personal conversations with seekers and lifelong believers.

They represent the questions people ask—not the ones theologians assume they should ask. Some questions probe profound theological truths, such as the nature of the Trinity or the meaning of salvation. Others deal with everyday concerns, including how to pray, overcome temptation, and make wise decisions. Questions about tough, sensitive issues—like the reality of suffering, the nature of hell, and apparent contradictions in Scripture—demand thoughtful, compassionate answers.

These questions reflect the real struggles and honest curiosity of everyday people, and this book seeks to answer them with both clarity and grace, rooted firmly in the wisdom of Scripture.

How to Use This Book

Each question stands on its own, making this book flexible in your needs. You can read from cover to cover for a comprehensive overview of Christian teaching, or you can turn directly to questions most relevant to your current circumstances or interests.

The answers include Scripture references, showing that these aren't just personal interpretations, but teachings grounded in God's Word. Key Bible verses are highlighted at the end of each answer, providing starting points for deeper study.

Throughout these pages, you'll find a consistent approach that is:

- Clear without oversimplifying
- Biblically faithful without being rigid
- Compassionate without compromising the truth
- Practical without being superficial

Remember that God isn't intimidated by your questions. He isn't surprised by your doubts or disappointed in your curiosity. The God who created the human mind welcomes our sincere seeking, knowing that as we search for answers, we're ultimately searching for Him.

My prayer is that through these pages, you'll discover not just information about God but a deeper relationship with Him. May these answers strengthen your faith, resolve your doubts, and draw you closer to the who says, "Ask and it will be given to you; seek, and you will find; knock and the door will be opened to you" (Matthew 7:7).

Let's begin this journey together.

Section 1: Understanding God

Question 1: Does God exist?

The Bible begins with a simple declaration: "In the beginning, God created..." (Genesis 1:1). This foundational truth serves as the starting point for all Scripture. While the Bible doesn't prove God's existence, it provides compelling evidence that He is real.

Look around at creation. The intricate design of the universe points to an intelligent Designer. As Psalm 19:1 tells us, "The heavens declare the glory of God; the skies proclaim the work of his hands." The complexity of DNA, the precision of planetary orbits, and the beauty of a sunset all whisper of Someone beyond ourselves.

Our innate moral compass also suggests a moral Lawgiver. Even without formal religious training, people across cultures share basic concepts of right and wrong. Romans 2:15 explains that God's law is "written on their hearts."

But God hasn't left us with only these hints. He has revealed Himself clearly through Scripture and ultimately through Jesus Christ, who showed us exactly what God is like. John 1:18 says, "No one has ever seen God, but the one and only Son...has made him known."

Believing in God requires faith, but it's not blind faith. Hebrews 11:6 reminds us, "Anyone who comes to Him must believe that He exists, and that He rewards those who earnestly seek Him." If you genuinely seek God, He promises you'll find Him.

Key Bible Verses:

- "In the beginning, God created the heavens and the earth." (Genesis 1:1)
- "The heavens declare the glory of God; the skies proclaim the work of his hands." (Psalm 19:1)
- "Anyone who comes to him must believe that he exists and that he rewards those who earnestly seek him." (Hebrews 11:6)

Question 2: What is God like?

God is greater and more wonderful than our minds can fully comprehend, yet He has revealed key aspects of His nature in Scripture. These attributes help us know who God is and how we can relate to Him.

First, God is spirit (John 4:24), eternal (Psalm 90:2), and unchanging (James 1:17). Unlike us, He has no beginning or end and exists beyond the limitations of time and space. He never grows tired or weak, and His character remains perfectly consistent.

God is all-powerful (omnipotent), knows everything (omniscient), and is present everywhere (omnipresent). Nothing is impossible for Him (Jeremiah 32:17), no thought escapes His notice (Psalm 139:1-4), and there's nowhere we can go beyond His presence (Psalm 139:7-10).

Most importantly, God is both holy and loving. His holiness means He is wholly pure and separate from all evil (Isaiah 6:3). His justice ensures that He always does what is right. Yet God is not distant—He is compassionate, merciful, and gracious. As 1 John 4:8 beautifully states, "God is love." This isn't just something He shows; it's who He is.

All these attributes work together in perfect harmony. In Jesus, we see God's attributes on full display—His power over nature, His holiness expressed in a sinless life, and His love showed through His sacrifice on our behalf.

Key Bible Verses:

- "God is spirit, and his worshipers must worship in the Spirit and in truth." (John 4:24)
- "Holy, holy, holy is the LORD Almighty; the whole earth is full of his glory." (Isaiah 6:3)
- "Whoever does not love does not know God, because God is love." (1 John 4:8)

Question 3: What is the Trinity?

The Trinity is the Christian teaching that one God eternally exists as three Persons: Father, Son, and Holy Spirit. Although the word "Trinity" does not appear in the Bible, the concept is deeply rooted in biblical teachings.

Scripture affirms that there is only one God (Deuteronomy 6:4). Yet the Bible also reveals that the Father is God, Jesus the Son is God, and the Holy Spirit is God. How can this be? The Trinity is not a contradiction, but a profound mystery that reflects God's complex nature.

The Father, Son, and Holy Spirit are distinct from one another, but perfectly united in essence and purpose. We see this beautifully displayed at Jesus' baptism: the Father speaks from heaven, the Son is baptized, and the Spirit descends like a dove (Matthew 3:16-17).

In the Great Commission, Jesus instructs his disciples to baptize "in the name of the Father and of the Son and of the Holy Spirit" (Matthew 28:19). Paul's blessing in 2 Corinthians 13:14 similarly references all three Persons: "May the grace of the Lord Jesus Christ, and the love of God, and the fellowship of the Holy Spirit be with you all."

While Trinity exceeds our complete comprehension, this shouldn't surprise us. As Isaiah 55:8-9 reminds us, God's thoughts and ways are higher than ours. The Trinity reveals a God who is inherently relational and loving within Himself—and amazingly, through Jesus, He invites us into that divine fellowship.

Key Bible Verses:

- "Hear, O Israel: The LORD our God, the LORD is one." (Deuteronomy 6:4)
- "Therefore go and make disciples of all nations, baptizing them in the name of the Father and of the Son and of the Holy Spirit." (Matthew 28:19)
- "May the grace of the Lord Jesus Christ, and the love of God, and the fellowship of the Holy Spirit be with you all." (2 Corinthians 13:14)

Question 4: Is God in control of everything?

Yes, God is sovereign, which means He has supreme authority and power over all creation. This biblical truth can bring great comfort, even when circumstances seem chaotic.

Scripture repeatedly affirms God's ultimate control. Daniel 4:35 declares, "He does as he pleases with the powers of heaven and the peoples of the earth. No one can hold back his hand." God's sovereignty extends over nature, nations, history, and individual lives.

This doesn't mean that God directly causes everything that happens. He has given humans genuine freedom to make choices, and much suffering results from our misuse of that freedom. Yet God is so wise and powerful that He can work even through human decisions—including sinful ones—to accomplish His purposes. Joseph recognized this when he tells his brothers, "You intended to harm me, but God intended it for good" (Genesis 50:20).

For believers, Romans 8:28 offers this excellent assurance: "We know that in all things God works for the good of those who love him, who have been called according to his purpose." God's sovereignty means nothing in this world—no tragedy, hardship, or enemy— beyond His ability to redeem and use for good.

Key Bible Verses:

- "The LORD does whatever pleases him, in the heavens and on the earth, in the seas and all their depths." (Psalm 135:6)

- "In him we were also chosen, having been predestined according to the plan of him who works out everything in conformity with the purpose of his will." (Ephesians 1:11)

- "And we know that in all things God works for the good of those who love him, who have been called according to his purpose." (Romans 8:28)

Question 5: Does God really love me?

It's normal to wonder if God truly loves you personally. The resounding answer from Scripture is yes—God's love for you is absolute, unconditional, and immeasurable.

The most powerful evidence of God's love is found in John 3:16: "For God so loved the world that he gave his one and only Son, that whoever believes in him shall not perish but have eternal life." You are included in that "world" that God loves. Romans 5:8 adds that "God demonstrates his love for us in this: While we were still sinners, Christ died for us." God didn't wait for you to be perfect—He loved you at your worst.

God's love isn't based on your performance or worthiness. It flows from His nature, because "God is love" (1 John 4:8). He loves you not because you've earned it, but because you are His creation and, in Christ, His beloved child. The apostle John marvels at this when he wrote, "See what great love the Father has lavished on us, that we should be called children of God! And that is what we are!" (1 John 3:1).

This love is steady and enduring. Nothing can separate you from it (Romans 8:38-39). Even when you feel unlovable or when life is difficult, God's care for you remains constant. Like a perfect parent, God may correct you when needed, but always in love—because He desires your best.

Key Bible Verses:

- "For God so loved the world that he gave his one and only Son, that whoever believes in him shall not perish but have eternal life." (John 3:16)
- "But God demonstrates his love for us in this: While we were still sinners, Christ died for us." (Romans 5:8)
- "See what great love the Father has lavished on us, that we should be called children of God! And that is what we are!" (1 John 3:1)

Question 6: Why did God create us?

God created humanity not out of loneliness or need, but out of love and for His glory. God is complete within Himself—Father, Son, and Holy Spirit—existing in perfect fellowship. He didn't need us, but He chose to create us to express His goodness.

Scripture tells us that humans were created in God's image (Genesis 1:27), designed to reflect His character and enjoy a relationship with Him. Isaiah 43:7 says we were created for God's glory. This doesn't mean God needed more praise; instead, He made us to experience the joy of knowing Him and reflecting His goodness in the world.

Unlike the rest of creation, humans were given the capacity for a relationship with God. He gave us the mind to know Him, hearts to love Him, and wills to choose Him. Sadly, humanity turned away through sin. Yet God's desire for a relationship never changed, so He sent Jesus to restore what was broken.

The wonder of creation is that God wanted you. You are not an accident. You were designed with a purpose: to know God, to enjoy Him, and to glorify Him through your life.

Key Bible Verses:

- "So God created mankind in his own image, in the image of God he created them; male and female he created them." (Genesis 1:27)
- "Everyone who is called by my name, whom I created for my glory, whom I formed and made." (Isaiah 43:7)
- "You are worthy, our Lord and God, to receive glory and honor and power, for you created all things, and by your will they were created and have their being." (Revelation 4:11)

Question 7: What does it mean that God is holy?

Holiness is perhaps the most fundamental attribute of God, yet it's often misunderstood. To say God is holy means He is wholly pure and utterly different from anything or anyone else. The Hebrew word for "holy" means "set apart" or "separate." God's holiness encompasses both His moral perfection and His transcendent nature.

In Isaiah's vision of God's throne, angels called to one another: "Holy, holy, holy is the LORD Almighty; the whole earth is full of his glory" (Isaiah 6:3). This triple repetition—unique in Scripture's description of God's attributes—emphasizes the centrality of holiness in God's character.

God's holiness helps us understand our need for grace. Compared to His absolute purity, our sinfulness becomes painfully clear. Isaiah responded to God's holiness: "Woe to me! I am ruined!" (Isaiah 6:5). Yet God doesn't leave us in our uncleanness. Through Christ's sacrifice, we can confidently approach the holy God (Hebrews 10:19-22).

God calls His people to reflect His holiness: "Be holy, because I am holy" (1 Peter 1:16). This doesn't mean sinless perfection, but a life increasingly separated from sin and dedicated to God. As we grow in Christ, we're being transformed into His image, reflecting more of His holy character.

Key Bible Verses:

- "Holy, holy, holy is the LORD Almighty; the whole earth is full of his glory." (Isaiah 6:3)
- "But just as he who called you is holy, so be holy in all you do." (1 Peter 1:15)
- "Make every effort to live in peace with everyone and to be holy; without holiness no one will see the Lord." (Hebrews 12:14)

Question 8: Can we know God personally?

Yes! Scripture teaches that God desires a personal relationship with us and has made it possible through Jesus Christ. From the beginning, God walked with Adam and Eve in close fellowship in the Garden of Eden. Though sin disrupted that intimacy, God immediately began working to restore it.

The entire Bible tells the story of God pursuing a relationship with humanity. He revealed Himself to Abraham, Moses, and the prophets. But his ultimate self-disclosure came through Jesus, who says, "Anyone who has seen me has seen the Father" (John 14:9). Jesus even defined eternal life not as living forever but as knowing God: "Now this is eternal life: that they know you, the only true God, and Jesus Christ, whom you have sent" (John 17:3).

Through Christ's death and resurrection, the barrier of sin has been removed. When we trust Jesus, we become God's children (John 1:12), adopted into His family with all the privileges of sonship or daughterhood. Knowing He welcomes us, we can confidently approach God (Hebrews 4:16).

This relationship is authentic and interactive. God speaks to us through Scripture and the guidance of the Holy Spirit. We talk to Him through prayer. As we draw near to God, He draws near to us (James 4:8), and this relationship grows deeper throughout our lives.

Key Bible Verses:

- "Now this is eternal life: that they know you, the only true God, and Jesus Christ, whom you have sent." (John 17:3)

- "Yet to all who did receive him, to those who believed in his name, he gave the right to become children of God." (John 1:12)
- "Come near to God and he will come near to you." (James 4:8)

Question 9: What does it mean to "fear God"?

The biblical concept of "fearing God" is often misunderstood. It doesn't mean being terrified of God as we might fear a tyrant or abuser. Instead, it combines deep reverence, awe, and respect with a healthy recognition of God's power and holiness.

Proverbs 9:10 says, "The fear of the LORD is the beginning of wisdom." This means that proper understanding of life begins when we grasp who God is—the Creator, Sustainer, and Judge of all. Proper fear acknowledges God's authority and righteousness. It's like how a child might "fear" a loving parent—not in terror, but in respectful recognition of their authority and wisdom.

This reverence affects how we live. It motivates us to obey God, not out of dread of punishment but out of a desire to honour the one we love and respect. Ecclesiastes 12:13 summarizes life's purpose: "Fear God and keep his commandments, for this is the duty of all mankind."

Remarkably, the Bible balances this fear with intimate trust. The same God who deserves our reverence also invites us to call Him "Abba, Father" (Romans 8:15)—an endearing term like "Daddy." Proper fear of God doesn't drive us away from Him but draws us closer in humble dependence and worship.

Key Bible Verses:

- "The fear of the LORD is the beginning of wisdom, and knowledge of the Holy One is understanding." (Proverbs 9:10)
- "Serve the LORD with fear and celebrate his rule with trembling." (Psalm 2:11)
- "His mercy extends to those who fear him, from generation to generation." (Luke 1:50)

Question 10: Who created God?

This question arises naturally when thinking about origins, but it misunderstands the nature of God as revealed in Scripture. The Bible teaches that God is eternal—without beginning or end. He wasn't created; He has always existed.

The concept of creation only applies to things that have a beginning. God, by definition, has no beginning. Psalm 90:2 declares, "Before the mountains were born or you brought forth the entire world, from everlasting to everlasting, you are God." The phrase "from everlasting to everlasting" shows that God's existence transcends time. He exists outside of time as his Creator.

The Bible begins simply with "In the beginning, God..." (Genesis 1:1). It assumes God's eternal existence as the starting point of everything else. In Revelation 1:8, God identifies Himself as "the Alpha and the Omega"—the beginning and end of the Greek alphabet—signifying He encompasses all reality.

"Who created God?" is like asking, "What is north of the North Pole?" It applies a category (creation) to One who transcends that category. God is the uncaused cause, the uncreated Creator. While our finite minds struggle to grasp this concept, it's because God is eternal and uncreated that He can be the ultimate foundation of everything else.

Key Bible Verses:

- "Before the mountains were born or you brought forth the whole world, from everlasting to everlasting you are God." (Psalm 90:2)

- "I am the Alpha and the Omega," says the Lord God, "who is, and who was, and who is to come, the Almighty." (Revelation 1:8)

- "In the beginning, God created the heavens and the earth." (Genesis 1:1)

Section 2: Jesus Christ

Question 11: Who is Jesus Christ?

Jesus Christ is the central figure of Christianity and one of the most influential people in history. The Bible reveals Him as fully God and human—a unique Person who entered our world to reveal God and provide salvation.

Jesus is God the Son, the second Person of the Trinity. John 1:1-14 states that "the Word was God" and then "became flesh and made his dwelling among us." Jesus Himself claimed equality with God (John 10:30), and His disciples recognized His deity (John 20:28). He demonstrated divine attributes, such as receiving worship, forgiving sins, and exercising power over nature, disease, and death.

Yet Jesus was also completely human. He experienced hunger, thirst, fatigue, joy, and sorrow. He grew in wisdom (Luke 2:52) and felt temptation (Hebrews 4:15), though He never sinned. This dual nature—fully God and fully man—uniquely qualified Him to be our Savior, mediating between God and humanity.

As Messiah (Christ means "anointed one"), Jesus fulfilled hundreds of Old Testament prophecies. Through His perfect life, sacrificial death, and resurrection, He accomplished God's plan of redemption. He now reigns at God's right hand and will return as King to establish God's kingdom fully.

Jesus isn't just a historical figure or religious teacher; He's the living Lord who offers a relationship with God to all who trust Him.

Key Bible Verses:

- "The Word became flesh and made his dwelling among us. We have seen his glory, the glory of the one and only Son, who came from the Father, full of grace and truth." (John 1:14)

- "For in Christ all the fullness of the Deity lives in bodily form." (Colossians 2:9)

- "For we do not have a high priest who is unable to empathize with our weaknesses, but we have one who has been tempted in every way, just as we are—yet he did not sin." (Hebrews 4:15)

Question 12: Is Jesus really God?

Yes, Jesus is truly God. This foundational truth distinguishes Christianity from other religions and is essential to our faith. While some may see Jesus as a good teacher or prophet, Scripture consistently affirms His divine nature.

Jesus repeatedly claimed equality with God. He declares, "I and the Father are one" (John 10:30) and "Before Abraham was born, I am!" (John 8:58)—using God's name from Exodus 3:14. When Thomas called Him "My Lord and my God," Jesus accepted this worship (John 20:28-29).

The apostles affirmed Jesus' deity throughout their writings. Paul wrote that "in Christ all the fullness of the Deity lives in bodily form" (Colossians 2:9). The book of Hebrews begins by stating that the Son is "the exact representation of [God's] being" (Hebrews 1:3).

Jesus demonstrated divine attributes, including omniscience (knowing people's thoughts), omnipotence (controlling nature), and the authority to forgive sins—attributes believed to be exclusive to God. He accepted worship, which would be blasphemy for a mere human.

This truth matters profoundly. If Jesus were just a good man, His death could not atone for our sins. Only God in human flesh could bear the weight of the world's sin. The incarnation—God becoming human—is the greatest miracle and the foundation of our hope.

Key Bible Verses:

- "In the beginning was the Word, and the Word was with God, and the Word was God." (John 1:1)
- "I and the Father are one." (John 10:30)
- "Thomas said to him, 'My Lord and my God!'" (John 20:28)

Question 13: Why did Jesus die on the cross?

Jesus died on the cross as the ultimate sacrifice for humanity's sins. This central event of history fulfilled God's plan to reconcile sinful humans to Himself while upholding His perfect justice.

The problem is our sin. All people have rebelled against God, violating His holy standards (Romans 3:23). This sin separates us from God. It deserves death—both physical and spiritual (Romans 6:23). God's justice requires that sin be punished, but His love desires our salvation.

Jesus provided the solution. As the sinless Son of God, He voluntarily took our place, bearing the punishment we deserved. Isaiah 53:5 prophesied this substitution: "He was pierced for our transgressions, he was crushed for our iniquities; the punishment that brought us peace was on him, and by his wounds we are healed."

On the cross, Jesus accomplished several things:

- He satisfied God's justice by paying sin's penalty (Romans 3:25-26)
- He demonstrated God's love (Romans 5:8)
- He defeated Satan and the powers of evil (Colossians 2:15)
- He provided forgiveness and reconciliation with God (2 Corinthians 5:18-19)

Jesus' sacrifice wasn't a tragic accident but God's deliberate plan (Acts 2:23). His death shows both the seriousness of sin and the depth of God's love. Through faith in Christ, we receive the benefits of His death—forgiveness, peace with God, and eternal life.

Key Bible Verses:

- "For God so loved the world that he gave his one and only Son, that whoever believes in him shall not perish but have eternal life." (John 3:16)

- "But God demonstrates his own love for us in this: While we were still sinners, Christ died for us." (Romans 5:8)

- "He himself bore our sins in his body on the cross, so that we might die to sins and live for righteousness; by his wounds you have been healed." (1 Peter 2:24)

Question 14: Did Jesus really rise from the dead?

Yes, Jesus' bodily resurrection is one of the most well-established events in ancient history and the cornerstone of Christian faith. As Paul wrote, "If Christ has not been raised, your faith is futile" (1 Corinthians 15:17). Thankfully, there is substantial evidence to support this miraculous event.

Multiple eyewitnesses saw the risen Christ. The Gospels record several appearances to individuals and groups. Paul states that Jesus appeared to more than 500 people at once, most of whom were still alive when he wrote (1 Corinthians 15:6), inviting skeptics to check his claim with living witnesses.

The empty tomb is compelling evidence. If Jesus' body remained in the grave, authorities could have easily silenced claims of resurrection by producing it. The fact that even Jesus' enemies had to invent stories to explain the empty tomb (Matthew 28:11-15) supports the reality of it.

The disciples' transformation also confirms the resurrection. These men went from hiding in fear to boldly proclaiming Christ's resurrection—even facing torture and death for this testimony. Such dramatic change makes sense only if they truly encountered the risen Jesus.

Finally, the explosive growth of the early Church in Jerusalem, where the resurrection claim could be easily investigated, suggests the evidence was convincing even to firsthand observers.

Jesus' resurrection validates His claims, confirms His deity, and guarantees our future resurrection. Because He lives, we can face tomorrow with confidence.

Key Bible Verses:

- "He is not here; he has risen, just as he said." (Matthew 28:6)

- "Christ died for our sins according to the Scriptures, that he was buried, that he was raised on the third day according to the Scriptures, and that he appeared to Cephas, and then to the Twelve." (1 Corinthians 15:3-5)

- "Because I live, you also will live." (John 14:19)

Question 15: What is salvation?

Salvation is God's rescue plan for humanity—Delivering us from sin and its consequences and restoring us to a relationship with Himself. This grand theme runs throughout Scripture and finds its fulfillment in Jesus Christ.

At its core, salvation addresses our most significant problem: separation from God due to sin. Sin has three terrible consequences: guilt (legal penalty), corruption (moral damage), and alienation (relational breach). Salvation reverses all three through justification (forgiveness of sins), sanctification (moral transformation), and reconciliation (restored relationship with God).

Salvation is entirely God's work, motivated by His love and grace. Ephesians 2:8-9 states, "For it is by grace you have been saved, through faith—and this is not from yourselves, it is the gift of God—not by works so that no one can boast." We can't earn salvation through good deeds or religious rituals; we can only receive it as a gift through faith in Christ.

This salvation affects every dimension of our lives. It changes our past (through forgiveness), our present (to a new life in Christ), and our future (to eternal hope). It transforms our identity, purpose, and destiny. Though its fullness awaits Christ's return, believers already enjoy its benefits as "new creation" (2 Corinthians 5:17).

Key Bible Verses:

- "For it is by grace you have been saved, through faith—and this is not from yourselves, it is the gift of God—not by works, so that no one can boast." (Ephesians 2:8-9)

- "For the wages of sin is death, but the gift of God is eternal life in Christ Jesus our Lord." (Romans 6:23)

- "Salvation is found in no one else, for there is no other name under heaven given to mankind by which we must be saved." (Acts 4:12)

Question 16: How can I be saved?

Being saved means being rescued from sin's penalty and power and receiving eternal life with God. The Bible presents a clear path to salvation that's simple enough for a child to understand yet profound enough to transform your entire life.

First, recognize your need for salvation. Romans 3:23 states, "All have sinned and fall short of the glory of God." We've all broken God's laws and stand guilty before Him. Our sin separates us from God and leads to spiritual death (Romans 6:23). Good works alone cannot get us to heaven (Ephesians 2:8-9).

Second, believe that Jesus Christ is God's provision for your salvation. Through His death on the cross, Jesus paid the penalty for your sins. Through His resurrection, He conquered death and offers new life. John 3:16 promises, "For God so loved the world that he gave his one and only Son, that whoever believes in him shall not perish but have eternal life."

Third, respond to God's offer with repentance and faith. Repentance means turning from sin and self-rule. Faith means trusting Christ alone for salvation. Romans 10:9 explains, "If you declare with your mouth, 'Jesus is Lord,' and believe in your heart that God raised him from the dead, you will be saved."

You can express this decision through a simple prayer but remember—it's not the words that save you, but the heart attitude of repentance and faith. God promises to save everyone who calls on Him (Romans 10:13).

Key Bible Verses:

- "For God so loved the world that he gave his one and only Son, that whoever believes in him shall not perish but have eternal life." (John 3:16)

- "If you declare with your mouth, 'Jesus is Lord,' and believe in your heart that God raised him from the dead, you will be saved." (Romans 10:9)

- "Everyone who calls on the name of the Lord will be saved." (Romans 10:13)

Question 17: What does it mean to be "born again"?

Jesus tells Nicodemus, "Very truly I tell you, no one can see the kingdom of God unless they are born again" (John 3:3). This puzzling statement describes a spiritual transformation that's essential for salvation.

To be "born again" means to experience a spiritual rebirth—a supernatural work of God where He gives new life to those who trust in Christ. Just as physical birth brings us into the physical world, spiritual birth brings us into God's family and kingdom.

We don't achieve this new birth through religious rituals or moral effort. Jesus explained to Nicodemus that it is a work of the Holy Spirit, as mysterious and sovereign as the wind (John 3:8). While we cannot control or manipulate this divine work, we must respond to it through faith in Christ.

When someone is born again, they become a "new creation" (2 Corinthians 5:17). The Holy Spirit indwells them, giving them new desires, perspectives, and power to live for God. This transformation doesn't make us instantly perfect, but it does begin a lifelong process of becoming more like Christ.

How can you tell if you've been born again? The evidence includes faith in Christ, a growing love for God and others, a decreasing hatred of sin, and a desire to obey God's Word. These aren't the cause of new birth but their natural fruits.

Key Bible Verses:

- "Jesus replied, 'Very truly I tell you, no one can see the kingdom of God unless they are born again.'" (John 3:3)

- "Therefore, if anyone is in Christ, the new creation has come: The old has gone, the new is here!" (2 Corinthians 5:17)

- "Everyone who believes that Jesus is the Christ is born of God." (1 John 5:1)

Question 18: Why is Jesus the only way to God?

In our pluralistic world, Jesus' claim to be the exclusive path to God can seem narrow-minded. Yet Jesus Himself says, "I am the way and the truth and the life. No one comes to the father except through me" (John 14:6). Why must we come to God through Jesus alone?

First, only Jesus addresses our fundamental problem: sin. All humans have rebelled against God (Romans 3:23), creating a separation that we cannot bridge ourselves. Other religions typically offer self-improvement systems, but Christianity recognizes that we need more than improvement—rescue.

Second, only Jesus provides a perfect sacrifice for sin. As both fully God and fully human, Jesus uniquely qualifies to mediate between God and humanity (1 Timothy 2:5). His sinless life and sacrificial death satisfy God's justice, paying a debt we could never pay ourselves.

Third, only Jesus conquered death through resurrection, demonstrating His divine authority and power to give eternal life. No other religious leader has overcome death; only Jesus emerged from the grave, proving His claims.

Fourth, only Jesus is God incarnate. While other religious teachers may offer wise teachings, Jesus affords Himself—God in human flesh, revealing the Father perfectly.

This exclusivity isn't based on cultural superiority but on Jesus' unique identity and work. It's not that Christianity arbitrarily rejects other paths; it's that Jesus alone provides what humans truly need: reconciliation with God through forgiving sins.

Key Bible Verses:

- "Jesus answered, 'I am the way and the truth and the life. No one comes to the Father except through me.'" (John 14:6)

- "Salvation is found in no one else, for there is no other name under heaven given to mankind by which we must be saved." (Acts 4:12)

- "For there is one God and one mediator between God and mankind, the man Christ Jesus." (1 Timothy 2:5)

Question 19: Can we earn salvation by good works?

This is one of the most common misconceptions people hold about salvation. The idea that "good people go to heaven" seems fair and logical to many. It aligns with how much of life works—effort gets rewarded, and failure gets punished. But when it comes to salvation, the Bible teaches something radically different.

Salvation is not something we can earn; it is a gift from God. Ephesians 2:8–9 clarifies this: "For it is by grace you have been saved, through faith—and this is not from yourselves, it is the gift of God—not by works so that no one can boast." No amount of kindness, charity, church attendance, or moral behaviour can earn us a place in heaven. Titus 3:5 echoes this: "He saved us, not because of righteous things we had done, but because of His mercy."

Why can't good works save us? Because God's standard is absolute perfection. James 2:10 explains, "For whoever keeps the whole law and yet stumbles at just one point is guilty of breaking all of it." None of us meets that standard—Romans 3:23 reminds us that "all have sinned and fall short of the glory of God." Even our best efforts are stained by imperfection when measured against God's holiness (Isaiah 64:6).

That's why we need grace. Jesus did what we could never do—He lived a sinless life and died in our place, taking the punishment, we deserved. When we trust Him, His righteousness is credited to us (2 Corinthians 5:21). Our salvation depends entirely on what Jesus has done, not on what we can do.

This doesn't mean that good work is unimportant. Instead, they are the *result* of salvation, not its requirement. A transformed life produces good fruit (Galatians 5:22–23), but that fruit is evidence of faith, not the means to obtain it. As believers, we are "created in Christ Jesus to do good works" (Ephesians 2:10), but only after we are saved by grace through faith.

Key Bible Verses:

- "For it is by grace you have been saved, through faith... not by works, so that no one can boast." (Ephesians 2:8–9)

- "He saved us, not because of righteous things we had done, but because of His mercy." (Titus 3:5)

- "All have sinned and fall short of the glory of God." (Romans 3:23)

- "Whoever keeps the whole law and yet stumbles at just one point is guilty of breaking all of it." (James 2:10)

- "God made him who had no sin to be sin for us, so that in him we might become the righteousness of God." (2 Corinthians 5:21)

Question 20: Did Jesus ever sin?

No, Jesus never sinned. While fully human and facing genuine temptation, He remained perfectly obedient to God throughout His life. This sinlessness is essential to His role as our Savior.

Scripture affirms Jesus' sinlessness repeatedly. Hebrews 4:15 states that Jesus "has been tempted in every way, just as we are—yet he did not sin." Peter, who lived with Jesus for three years, testified that Jesus "committed no sin, and no deceit was found in his mouth" (1 Peter 2:22). Even Jesus' enemies struggled to find legitimate accusations against Him.

Jesus' sinlessness wasn't automatic or effortless. As a real human, He faced authentic temptation, including Satan's direct enticements in the wilderness (Matthew 4:1-11). Yet through dependence on the Father and the Spirit, Jesus remained faithful.

Why does this matter? First, only a sinless sacrifice could atone for our sins. Just as Old Testament sacrifices had to be "without defect," Jesus had to be without moral blemish to bear our sins (2 Corinthians 5:21).

Second, Jesus' sinless life provides both inspiration and help for our struggles. He understands our temptations from experience yet shows that the power of God can overcome sin. And His perfect obedience is credited to believers, clothing us with His righteousness (Romans 5:19).

Key Bible Verses:

- "For we do not have a high priest who is unable to empathize with our weaknesses, but we have one who has been tempted in every way, just as we are—yet he did not sin." (Hebrews 4:15)

- "God made him who had no sin to be sin for us, so that in him we might become the righteousness of God." (2 Corinthians 5:21)

- "He committed no sin, and no deceit was found in his mouth." (1 Peter 2:22)

Section 3: The Holy Spirit

Question 21: Who is the Holy Spirit?

The Holy Spirit is the third Person of the Trinity—fully God, equal with the Father and the Son. He is not an impersonal force or energy, but a divine Person who thinks, feels, and acts.

When Jesus prepared His disciples for His departure, He promises to send "another advocate" or "helper" (John 14:16)—the Holy Spirit—who would continue His work. The Greek word "another" indicates someone of the same kind, showing the Holy Spirit's equality with Jesus. Throughout Scripture, the Holy Spirit is described with personal attributes: He speaks (Acts 13:2), teaches (John 14:26), can be grieved (Ephesians 4:30), and makes decisions (1 Corinthians 12:11).

The Holy Spirit was active in creation (Genesis 1:2), inspired the writing of Scripture (2 Peter 1:21), empowered Jesus during His earthly ministry (Luke 4:18), and was poured out on the church at Pentecost (Acts 2). Today, He lives within every believer (1 Corinthians 6:19), performing vital ministries including conviction of sin, guidance into truth, and character transformation.

Through the Holy Spirit, we experience God's presence, power, and help daily. He is God with us and in us, the divine Person who makes the Christian life possible.

Key Bible Verses:

- "And I will ask the Father, and he will give you another advocate to help you and be with you forever—the Spirit of truth." (John 14:16-17)

- "Do you not know that your bodies are temples of the Holy Spirit, who is in you, whom you have received from God?" (1 Corinthians 6:19)

- "But when he, the Spirit of truth, comes, he will guide you into all the truth." (John 16:13)

Question 22: Is the Holy Spirit God?

Yes, the Holy Spirit is fully God—equal in essence and divinity with the Father and the Son. This truth is vital for understanding how God works in our lives today.

Scripture affirms the deity of the Holy Spirit in various ways. In Acts 5:3-4, Peter tells Ananias that he lied to the Holy Spirit and then immediately says he lied "to God," showing their equivalence. The Holy Spirit possesses divine attributes like eternality (Hebrews 9:14), omniscience (1 Corinthians 2:10-11), and omnipresence (Psalm 139:7-10).

The Holy Spirit appears alongside the Father and Son in contexts emphasizing divinity, such as the baptismal formula (Matthew 28:19) and apostolic blessings (2 Corinthians 13:14). He performs divine works, including creation (Genesis 1:2), giving life (John 6:63), and inspiring Scripture (2 Peter 1:21).

This isn't just a theological technicality. Recognizing the Holy Spirit as God helps us approach Him with proper reverence and trust His work in our lives. When the Spirit guides us, it's God Himself directing our paths. When He empowers us, it's God's strength working through us. The indwelling Spirit isn't just a divine influence but the presence of God Himself within us—an astounding privilege and responsibility.

Key Bible Verses:

- "Then Peter said, 'Ananias, how is it that Satan has so filled your heart that you have lied to the Holy Spirit... You have not lied just to human beings but to God.'" (Acts 5:3-4)

- "Go and make disciples of all nations, baptizing them in the name of the Father and of the Son and of the Holy Spirit." (Matthew 28:19)

- "How much more, then, will the blood of Christ, who through the eternal Spirit offered himself unblemished to God, cleanse our consciences from acts that lead to death." (Hebrews 9:14)

Question 23: What does the Holy Spirit do?

The Holy Spirit performs numerous vital ministries both in the world and in the lives of believers. Understanding His work helps us cooperate with Him and experience the fullness of Christian life.

For unbelievers, the Holy Spirit "convicts the world concerning sin, righteousness, and judgment" (John 16:8). He opens spiritual eyes to see the truth about Jesus and draws people to salvation.

When someone puts their faith in Christ, the Holy Spirit:

- Regenerates them, giving spiritual rebirth (Titus 3:5)

- Baptizes them into the body of Christ (1 Corinthians 12:13)

- Indwells them permanently (Romans 8:9-11)

- Seals them as God's possession (Ephesians 1:13-14)

Throughout the Christian life, the Holy Spirit:

- Transforms believers into Christ's likeness (2 Corinthians 3:18)
- Empowers for holy living and service (Acts 1:8; Galatians 5:16)
- Guides into truth through Scripture (John 16:13)
- Helps in prayer, even interceding when we don't know how to pray (Romans 8:26)
- Distributes spiritual gifts for serving the church (1 Corinthians 12:4-11)
- Produces spiritual fruit—love, joy, peace, etc. (Galatians 5:22-23)
- Provides assurance of salvation (Romans 8:16)

The Holy Spirit's work touches every aspect of the Christian experience, from salvation to sanctification to eventual glorification. While he sometimes works dramatically, he often operates gently and quietly, always pointing to Jesus rather than himself (John 16:14).

Key Bible Verses:

- "But the Advocate, the Holy Spirit, whom the Father will send in my name, will teach you all things and will remind you of everything I have said to you." (John 14:26)
- "The Spirit himself testifies with our spirit that we are God's children." (Romans 8:16)
- "But the fruit of the Spirit is love, joy, peace, forbearance, kindness, goodness, faithfulness, gentleness and self-control." (Galatians 5:22-23)

Question 24: What are the gifts of the Holy Spirit?

Spiritual gifts are special abilities given by the Holy Spirit to equip believers to serve God and build up the church. These gifts reflect God's grace and are meant for the common good, not individual glory.

Scripture contains several lists of spiritual gifts (Romans 12:6-8; 1 Corinthians 12:8-10, 28-30; Ephesians 4:11; 1 Peter 4:10-11), including gifts like teaching, serving, giving, leadership, wisdom, faith, healing, prophecy, and discernment. No list is exhaustive, and the Spirit may work in ways beyond these specific categories.

Some key principles about spiritual gifts include:

- Every believer has at least one gift (1 Corinthians 12:7)
- Gifts are distributed according to God's sovereign choice, not our merit (1 Corinthians 12:11)
- No single gift is given to all believers (1 Corinthians 12:29-30)
- Gifts differ in function but are equally valuable (1 Corinthians 12:14-26)
- Gifts should be exercised in love (1 Corinthians 13:1-3)

- Gifts are for serving others, not self-promotion (1 Peter 4:10)

Christians sometimes debate whether certain miraculous gifts (like tongues, prophecy, or healing) continue today or ended with the apostolic era. Regardless of one's position on this question, all believers should discover, develop, and use the gifts God has given them for His glory and the benefit of others.

Key Bible Verses:

- "There are different kinds of gifts, but the same Spirit distributes them." (1 Corinthians 12:4)
- "Now to each one the manifestation of the Spirit is given for the common good." (1 Corinthians 12:7)
- "Each of you should use whatever gift you have received to serve others, as faithful stewards of God's grace in its various forms." (1 Peter 4:10)

Question 25: What is the fruit of the Spirit?

The fruit of the Spirit refers to the Christ-like character qualities that the Holy Spirit develops in believers. Galatians 5:22-23 lists nine aspects of this fruit: love, joy, peace, patience, kindness, goodness, faithfulness, gentleness, and self-control.

Unlike spiritual gifts, which differ among believers, the fruit of the Spirit is expected in every Christian's life. This fruit isn't produced through human effort alone but results from abiding in Christ (John 15:5) and walking by the Spirit (Galatians 5:16). It is the outward evidence of an inward transformation.

Several observations about this fruit are essential:

- It's singular "fruit" (not "fruits"), suggesting these qualities come as a package
- It reflects Jesus' character—we become more like Him
- It contrasts sharply with the "acts of the flesh" listed in Galatians 5:19-21
- It grows gradually, not instantly, like natural fruit
- It requires cultivation through spiritual disciplines and obedience
- It's for God's glory, not our reputation

The fruit of the Spirit isn't about perfection but direction. These qualities become increasingly natural as we yield to the Spirit's work. This transformation affects our relationship with God (love, joy, faithfulness), with others (patience, kindness, goodness, gentleness), and with ourselves (peace, self-control).

Key Bible Verses:

- "But the fruit of the Spirit is love, joy, peace, patience, kindness, goodness, faithfulness, gentleness and self-control." (Galatians 5:22-23)

- "I am the vine; you are the branches. If you remain in me and I in you, you will bear much fruit; apart from me you can do nothing." (John 15:5)
- "Walk by the Spirit, and you will not gratify the desires of the flesh." (Galatians 5:16)

Question 26: What does it mean to be filled with the Holy Spirit?

Scripture commands believers to "be filled with the Spirit" (Ephesians 5:18). This vital teaching concerns how we experience the Holy Spirit's power and influence in daily life.

The filling of the Spirit differs from the indwelling of the Spirit. All Christians are indwelt by the Spirit from the moment of salvation (Romans 8:9)—this is a permanent reality. Being filled, however, refers to the degree to which the Spirit controls and empowers us—this can fluctuate based on our responsiveness to Him.

The Greek verb for "be filled" in Ephesians 5:18 indicates an ongoing process, not a one-time event. It's also a command that shows our responsibility to seek this filing. The passage contrasts being drunk on wine with being filled with the Spirit—both influence behaviour, but in very different ways.

Being filled with the Spirit produces:

- Joyful worship and gratitude (Ephesians 5:19-20)
- Humble relationships with others (Ephesians 5:21)
- Boldness in witness (Acts 4:31)
- Wisdom and insight (Acts 6:3)
- Christlike character (Galatians 5:22-23)

How can we be filled? Through surrender (yielding control to God), confession of sin (which grieves the Spirit), obedience to God's Word, prayer for filling, and active trust in the Spirit's presence and power. This isn't about getting more of the Spirit but about the Spirit getting more of us.

Key Bible Verses:

- "Do not get drunk on wine, which leads to debauchery. Instead, be filled with the Spirit." (Ephesians 5:18)
- "After they prayed, the place where they were meeting was shaken. And they were all filled with the Holy Spirit and spoke the word of God boldly." (Acts 4:31)
- "Since we live by the Spirit, let us keep in step with the Spirit." (Galatians 5:25)

Question 27: What is the baptism of the Holy Spirit?

The baptism of the Holy Spirit is the act by which believers are placed into the body of Christ at the moment of salvation. This spiritual reality unites us with Christ and other believers in His church.

In 1 Corinthians 12:13, Paul states, "For we were all baptized by one Spirit to form one body—whether Jews or Gentiles, slave or free—and we were all given the one Spirit to drink." This verse shows that Spirit baptism is universal for all Christians, not a separate experience after salvation.

Before Jesus' ascension, He promised His disciples, "You will be baptized with the Holy Spirit" (Acts 1:5). This was fulfilled at Pentecost (Acts 2) when the Spirit first came to indwell believers and create the church. Today, this baptism occurs at conversion, as Peter indicates in Acts 2:38.

Some Christian traditions distinguish between conversion and the baptism of the Holy Spirit, viewing the latter as a separate experience often accompanied by speaking in tongues. However, while believers may have powerful experiences with the Spirit throughout their Christian life, Scripture consistently presents Spirit baptism as an initial work that includes all believers.

The baptism of the Holy Spirit gives us a new identity in Christ, spiritual empowerment, and connection to the global and historical body of believers. It's not something we need to seek after salvation—it's a blessing we've already received in Christ.

Key Bible Verses:

- "For we were all baptized by one Spirit so as to form one body—whether Jews or Gentiles, slave or free—and we were all given the one Spirit to drink." (1 Corinthians 12:13)
- "Repent and be baptized, every one of you, in the name of Jesus Christ for the forgiveness of your sins. And you will receive the gift of the Holy Spirit." (Acts 2:38)
- "If anyone does not have the Spirit of Christ, they do not belong to Christ." (Romans 8:9)

Question 28: How does the Holy Spirit guide us?

One of the Holy Spirit's most precious ministries is guidance. Jesus called Him "the Spirit of truth" who "will guide you into all the truth" (John 16:13). This guidance helps us navigate life according to God's will.

The Holy Spirit guides us in several ways:

First and foremost, through Scripture. The Spirit inspired the Bible (2 Peter 1:21) and illuminates our understanding. He never leads contrary to God's written Word but helps us apply its principles to specific situations.

Second, through the inner prompting of our conscience and spiritual intuition. Romans 8:14 says, "Those who are led by the Spirit of God are the children of God." This might involve a sense of peace or caution about a decision (Colossians 3:15).

Third, through the counsel of godly people. Proverbs affirm that "plans fail for lack of counsel" (Proverbs 15:22). The Spirit often speaks through mature believers who know Scripture and care about your spiritual welfare.

Fourth, through circumstances and open or closed doors. While we shouldn't base decisions solely on circumstances, God sometimes clearly directs through providential timing and opportunities.

Discerning the Spirit's guidance requires spiritual sensitivity, which is developed through prayer, studying Scripture, and gaining experience. It's also essential to test impressions against Scripture, wise counsel, and the Spirit's known character. The goal isn't just to know God's plan but to know God Himself better through the journey of seeking His direction.

Key Bible Verses:

- "But when he, the Spirit of truth, comes, he will guide you into all the truth." (John 16:13)
- "For those who are led by the Spirit of God are the children of God." (Romans 8:14)
- "Whether you turn to the right or to the left, your ears will hear a voice behind you, saying, 'This is the way; walk in it.'" (Isaiah 30:21)

Question 29: What does it mean to walk in the Spirit?

Paul instructs believers to "walk by the Spirit" (Galatians 5:16) or "keep in step with the Spirit" (Galatians 5:25). This metaphor of walking describes how Christians should live daily under the Holy Spirit's guidance and empowerment.

Walking in the Spirit means allowing the Holy Spirit to momentarily direct and empower your life. It's choosing to follow His leading rather than the impulses of our sinful nature. Paul promises that when we walk by the Spirit, we "will not gratify the desires of the flesh" (Galatians 5:16).

This spiritual walk involves several practical elements:

- Being continually filled with the Spirit (Ephesians 5:18)
- Regularly feeding on God's Word (Colossians 3:16)
- Promptly confessing and turning from sin (1 John 1:9)
- Consciously depending on the Spirit's power, not self-effort
- Being sensitive to the Spirit's promptings
- Surrendering your will to God's direction

Walking in the Spirit isn't mystical or complicated. It's consciously acknowledging your dependence on God throughout ordinary activities. It's saying, "Lord, I need Your wisdom for this decision," "Spirit, empower me to resist this temptation," or "Help me respond to this person with Your love."

The results of this Spirit-led Walk include growing freedom from sinful patterns, increasing Christlike character (the fruit of the Spirit), and a life that glorifies God and blesses others.

Key Bible Verses:

- "So I say, walk by the Spirit, and you will not gratify the desires of the flesh." (Galatians 5:16)
- "Since we live by the Spirit, let us keep in step with the Spirit." (Galatians 5:25)
- "Those who live according to the flesh have their minds set on what the flesh desires; but those who live by the Spirit have their minds set on what the Spirit desires." (Romans 8:5)

Question 30: What is the blasphemy of the Holy Spirit?

Few scriptural concepts have caused more anxiety than Jesus' warning about "blasphemy against the Holy Spirit" (Matthew 12:31-32)—the one sin He called unforgivable. Understanding this teaching correctly can relieve unnecessary fear.

The context is crucial. Religious leaders had just attributed Jesus' miracle of casting out demons to Satan's power, not God's Spirit. Jesus warned that this blasphemy "will not be forgiven, either in this age or in the age to come" (Matthew 12:32).

Blasphemy against the Holy Spirit is not a momentary lapse or casual sin. It involves:

- Deliberate, persistent rejection of the Spirit's witness about Christ
- Attributing the Spirit's work to evil sources
- Hardened, willful resistance to the truth
- Sustained unbelief with full knowledge

This sin is unforgivable not because God's grace has limits but because a person committing it has completely closed themselves to the only means of forgiveness—the Spirit's work in bringing people to Christ.

Importantly, those who worry they've committed this sin almost certainly haven't. Such concern shows spiritual sensitivity, not hardened rejection. People who have committed this sin wouldn't care about it, having moved beyond conviction. As Charles Spurgeon says, "No man can have committed the unpardonable sin while he has enough of the grace of God left to tremble at the thought of having committed it."

If you're concerned, take heart—your concern is evidence that your heart remains open to the Spirit.

Key Bible Verses:

- "Anyone who speaks a word against the Son of Man will be forgiven, but anyone who speaks against the Holy Spirit will not be forgiven, either in this age or in the age to come." (Matthew 12:32)

- "If we confess our sins, he is faithful and just and will forgive us our sins and purify us from all unrighteousness." (1 John 1:9)
- "Everyone who calls on the name of the Lord will be saved." (Romans 10:13)

Section 4: Sin and the Human Condition

Question 31: What is sin?

Sin is one of the Bible's most important concepts because it explains the brokenness in our world and our need for salvation. Sin is rebellion against God—any thought, word, action, or omission that violates His holy character and will.

The primary Hebrew and Greek words for sin in Scripture convey the idea of "missing the mark"—falling short of God's perfect standard. Romans 3:23 states that "all have sinned and fall short of the glory of God." Sin isn't just breaking arbitrary rules; it violates the moral law reflecting God's holy character.

Sin takes many forms—from deliberate disobedience to passive neglect of what's right. It includes actions and attitudes, what we do and fail to do. James 4:17 explains, "If anyone, then, knows the good they ought to do and doesn't do it, it is sin for them."

Sin began in the garden when Adam and Eve disobeyed God's command (Genesis 3). That initial rebellion corrupted human nature and affected all creation. Now, everyone inherits a sinful nature (Psalm 51:5) and commits individual sins.

Understanding sin helps us grasp our need for Christ. Sin isn't just a moral failure; it's a broken relationship with our Creator that only Jesus can restore through His death and resurrection.

Key Bible Verses:

- "Everyone who sins breaks the law; in fact, sin is lawlessness." (1 John 3:4)
- "For all have sinned and fall short of the glory of God." (Romans 3:23)
- "If we claim to be without sin, we deceive ourselves, and the truth is not in us." (1 John 1:8)

Question 32: Are all sins equal in God's eyes?

Some Christians claim all sins are equal to God, often quoting James 2:10: "Whoever keeps the whole law and yet stumbles at just one point is guilty of breaking all of it." But does Scripture truly teach that all sins are identical in God's sight?

In one sense, any sin—regardless of its nature—renders us guilty before God and in need of salvation. Even one transgression breaks our relationship with a holy God. In this legal or judicial sense, all sins equally condemn us.

However, Scripture indicates that sins differ in severity and consequence:

- Jesus spoke of "the least of these commandments" (Matthew 5:19), suggesting degrees of importance
- He tells Pilate that "the one who handed me over to you is guilty of a greater sin" (John 19:11)

- Jesus mentioned "weightier matters of the law" (Matthew 23:23)
- Some sins produce more serious earthly consequences than others
- Certain sins receive stricter judgment (James 3:1; Luke 12:47-48)

The Bible distinguishes between sins committed in ignorance and those done with full knowledge, between momentary weakness and persistent rebellion. Scripture also indicates more severe consequences for sins that cause others to sin (Mark 9:42).

This balanced understanding helps us avoid two errors: minimizing the seriousness of sin on the one hand or creating a hierarchy that excuses "lesser" sins on the other. All sin separates us from God and requires Christ's atoning sacrifice, yet we should recognize that some sins cause deeper damage to ourselves and others.

Key Bible Verses:

- "Whoever keeps the whole law and yet stumbles at just one point is guilty of breaking all of it." (James 2:10)
- "Jesus said, 'The one who handed me over to you is guilty of a greater sin.'" (John 19:11)
- "If anyone causes one of these little ones—those who believe in me—to stumble, it would be better for them if a large millstone were hung around their neck and they were thrown into the sea." (Mark 9:42)

Question 33: What is original sin?

Original sin refers to the fallen condition and sinful nature that all humans inherit from Adam and Eve after their disobedience in the Garden of Eden. This doctrine helps explain why sin is a universal part of the human experience—why even young children exhibit selfishness without being taught.

When Adam sinned as humanity's representative, he brought corruption and guilt to the entire human race. Romans 5:12 explains, "Sin entered the world through one man, and death through sin, and in this way, death came to all people because all sinned." We inherit both a corrupted nature inclined toward sin and legal guilt before God.

David acknowledged this inherited sinfulness when he wrote, "Surely I was sinful at birth, sinful from the time my mother conceived me" (Psalm 51:5). We don't become sinners when we first disobey; instead, we disobey because we are already sinners by nature.

Original sin affects every part of our being—intellect, emotions, will, and physical bodies. This doesn't mean we're as bad as we could be, but that no part of us remains untouched by sin's influence. Theologians call this "total depravity"—not that we're utterly depraved but thoroughly affected by sin.

This sobering doctrine highlights our desperate need for salvation. We need more than improvement or education—we need regeneration and forgiveness, which can only come through Christ, the "last Adam" who reverses the effects of the first Adam's sin (1 Corinthians 15:45-49).

Key Bible Verses:

- "Therefore, just as sin entered the world through one man, and death through sin, and in this way death came to all people because all sinned." (Romans 5:12)

- "Surely I was sinful at birth, sinful from the time my mother conceived me." (Psalm 51:5)

- "For as in Adam all die, so in Christ all will be made alive." (1 Corinthians 15:22)

Question 34: What are the consequences of sin?

Sin may seem momentarily pleasurable or harmless, but its consequences are devastating and far-reaching. Understanding the effects of sin helps us grasp its seriousness and our need for Christ.

The primary consequence of sin is spiritual death—separation from God. Isaiah 59:2 states, "Your iniquities have separated you from your God." This broken relationship with our Creator is sin's most profound tragedy.

Sin also brings guilt and shame. Adam and Eve immediately experienced shame after sinning, hiding from God and covering themselves (Genesis 3:7-8). We similarly experience the burden of a guilty conscience, which Paul describes as "the law written on our hearts" (Romans 2:15).

Physically, sin introduced death, disease, and suffering into God's perfect creation (Romans 5:12). The ground was cursed, making work toilsome (Genesis 3:17-19). Our bodies experience the effects of living in a fallen world.

Relationally, sin damages our connections with others through selfishness, anger, dishonesty, and other destructive behaviours. This began with Adam blaming Eve for his sin (Genesis 3:12) and continues in broken relationships today.

Eternally, without Christ's intervention, sin leads to final judgment and separation from God (Revelation 20:11-15).

The good news is that Jesus came to address all these consequences. Through His death and resurrection, He offers forgiveness, reconciliation with God, healing for relationships, and eventual restoration of all creation. While we still experience the temporal effects of sins, their eternal penalties have been paid for those who trust in Christ.

Key Bible Verses:

- "For the wages of sin is death, but the gift of God is eternal life in Christ Jesus our Lord." (Romans 6:23)

- "Your iniquities have separated you from your God; your sins have hidden his face from you, so that he will not hear." (Isaiah 59:2)

- "Do not be deceived: God cannot be mocked. A man reaps what he sows." (Galatians 6:7)

Question 35: Can sin be forgiven?

Yes, sin can be forgiven entirely through Jesus Christ. This is the heart of the gospel—God offers forgiveness to all who trust in His Son.

The depth of God's forgiveness is remarkable. No sin is too great or too many to be forgiven. Isaiah 1:18 promises, "Though your sins are like scarlet, they shall be as white as snow." Psalm 103:12 adds that God removes our sins "as far as the east is from the west." When God forgives, He chooses not to remember our sins anymore (Hebrews 8:12).

This forgiveness isn't easy or automatic. It required the sacrifice of Jesus Christ, who bore our sins on the cross. First, Peter 2:24 explains, "He himself bore our sins in his body on the cross." God's forgiveness perfectly balances justice (sin's penalty is paid) and mercy (we receive pardon we don't deserve).

To receive this forgiveness, we must:

- Acknowledge our sin honestly (1 John 1:8)
- Confess it to God (1 John 1:9)
- Turn from sin in repentance (Acts 3:19)
- Trust in Christ's sacrifice for our forgiveness (Romans 3:25)

When we do this, forgiveness is immediate and complete. While we may still face earthly consequences of our actions, our eternal standing with God is secure. As believers, if we continue to sin, we should continue to confess—not to be saved again, but to maintain close fellowship with God.

God's forgiveness becomes the model for forgiving others who wrong us (Ephesians 4:32).

Key Bible Verses:

- "If we confess our sins, he is faithful and just and will forgive us our sins and purify us from all unrighteousness." (1 John 1:9)
- "As far as the east is from the west, so far has he removed our transgressions from us." (Psalm 103:12)
- "In him we have redemption through his blood, the forgiveness of sins, in accordance with the riches of God's grace." (Ephesians 1:7)

Question 36: Why do we keep struggling with sin, even after salvation?

Many Christians are surprised—and often discouraged—by the ongoing presence of sin in their lives after coming to faith. They ask, "If I'm saved and forgiven, why do I still battle the same temptations, thoughts, or habits? Shouldn't salvation bring immediate victory?"

This struggle is not only common; it's biblical. The apostle Paul himself wrestled with this tension. In Romans 7:15 he writes, *"I do not understand what I do. For what I want to do, I do not do, but what I hate I do."* These words resonate with every believer who desires holiness but often falls short of it. Even Paul, one of the most influential leaders in church history, experienced the same internal war.

Here's why: salvation is both a moment and a process. When you put your faith in Jesus, you are immediately justified—declared righteous before God (Romans 5:1). You are also regenerated—given new spiritual life through the Holy Spirit (Titus 3:5). However, the transformation doesn't stop there. Sanctification—the lifelong journey of becoming more like Christ—takes time (Philippians 1:6). It involves learning, surrendering, failing, repenting, and growing.

While your spirit is made new, your old sinful nature (often called "the flesh") still lingers (Galatians 5:17). The Christian life is, therefore, a battle between the desires of the flesh and the leading of the Spirit. But this struggle is not a sign of failure—it's evidence that the Spirit is at work in you, drawing you toward righteousness.

Victory over sin is not about achieving perfection in this life but about pursuing Christ daily. Through prayer, Scripture, accountability, and the power of the Holy Spirit, we gradually grow stronger, and sin loses its grip. Some battles may persist longer than others, but the promise remains: God faithfully shapes you, even in your weakness (2 Corinthians 12:9).

Key Bible Verses:

- *"For the flesh desires what is contrary to the Spirit… They conflict with each other."* (Galatians 5:17)

- *"He who began a good work in you will carry it on to completion."* (Philippians 1:6)

- *"I do not do the good I want to do, but the evil I do not want to do—this I keep on doing."* (Romans 7:19)

- *"If we confess our sins, he is faithful and just and will forgive us."* (1 John 1:9)

Question 37: What is repentance?

Repentance is a foundational biblical concept that involves a heartfelt turning from sin toward God. It's far more than feeling sorry for wrongdoing—it's a complete change of mind, heart, and direction.

The Greek word for repentance, metanoia, literally means "to change one's mind." True repentance includes:

- Intellectual recognition of sin

- Emotional sorrow over sin

- Volitional turning from sin to God

Scripture distinguishes between "godly sorrow" (genuine repentance) and "worldly sorrow" (mere regret). As 2 Corinthians 7:10 explains, "Godly sorrow brings repentance that leads to salvation and leaves no regret, but worldly sorrow brings death." Worldly sorrow regrets consequences: godly sorrow grieves the sin itself.

Repentance isn't a one-time event but a lifestyle. Even as believers, we continue to repent as the Holy Spirit reveals areas that need change. This ongoing repentance deepens our relationship with God and increasingly aligns our lives with His will.

Importantly, repentance isn't about earning God's favour but responding to His grace already offered in Christ. It doesn't cause God to love us more; it opens our hearts to experience His love deeply. Throughout Scripture, God responds to genuine repentance with forgiveness, restoration, and blessing.

Key Bible Verses:

- "Repent, then, and turn to God, so that your sins may be wiped out, that times of refreshing may come from the Lord." (Acts 3:19)

- "Godly sorrow brings repentance that leads to salvation and leaves no regret, but worldly sorrow brings death." (2 Corinthians 7:10)

- "The Lord is not slow in keeping his promise, as some understand slowness. Instead he is patient with you, not wanting anyone to perish, but everyone to come to repentance." (2 Peter 3:9)

Question 38: What is temptation, and is it a sin?

Temptation itself is not sin—it's the enticement to sin. The distinction is crucial because many Christians unnecessarily feel guilty over being tempted when temptation is a regular part of the Christian experience.

Jesus Himself was "tempted in every way, just as we are—yet he did not sin" (Hebrews 4:15). This shows that experiencing temptation doesn't indicate spiritual failure. The temptation becomes sin only when we embrace it inwardly or act on it outwardly.

James 1:13-15 outlines the progression: "When tempted, no one should say, 'God is tempting me.' God cannot be tempted by evil, nor does he tempt anyone, but each person is tempted when they are dragged away by their evil desire and enticed. Then, after desire has conceived, it gives birth to sin; and sin, when it is full-grown, gives birth to death."

Temptation often targets legitimate needs or desires but suggests fulfilling them in ways that go beyond God's boundaries. It commonly appeals to pride, pleasure, or possessions—the same categories Satan used when tempting Jesus (Matthew 4:1-11).

When facing temptation, remember:

- God always provides a way of escape (1 Corinthians 10:13)

- Scripture is a powerful weapon against temptation (Ephesians 6:17)

- Prayer strengthens us before and during temptation (Matthew 26:41)

- Avoid situations that trigger your specific weaknesses

- Jesus understands your struggle and offers grace to help (Hebrews 4:15-16)

Rather than feeling shame over being tempted, view each temptation as an opportunity to demonstrate your love for God through obedience.

Key Bible Verses:

- "No temptation has overtaken you except what is common to mankind. And God is faithful; he will not let you be tempted beyond what you can bear. But when you are tempted, he will also provide a way out so that you can endure it." (1 Corinthians 10:13)
- "Each person is tempted when they are dragged away by their evil desire and enticed." (James 1:14)
- "For we do not have a high priest who is unable to empathize with our weaknesses, but we have one who has been tempted in every way, just as we are—yet he did not sin." (Hebrews 4:15)

Question 39: What is the unpardonable sin?

Few teachings have caused more anxiety than Jesus' warning about "blasphemy against the Holy Spirit"—the one sin He identified as unforgivable (Matthew 12:31-32). Understanding this properly can relieve unnecessary fear many Christians experience.

The context is vital. Jesus had just performed a miracle, casting out a demon by the power of the Holy Spirit. Instead of recognizing God's work, the Pharisees attributed it to Satan: "It is only by Beelzebul, the prince of demons, that this fellow drives out demons" (Matthew 12:24). Jesus then warned them about blaspheming the Holy Spirit.

Based on this context and other Scripture, blasphemy against the Holy Spirit appears to be:

- The deliberate, persistent rejection of the Holy Spirit's testimony about Christ
- Attributing the Spirit's work to evil sources while knowing better
- A settled, willful refusal to believe in Christ despite clear evidence
- Not a momentary lapse but a hardened heart condition

This sin is "unpardonable" not because it exceeds God's grace but because a person committing it has completely closed themselves to the only means of receiving forgiveness—the Spirit's work in bringing people to faith in Christ.

If you're worried you've committed this sin, that concern is evidence you haven't. Those who commit the unpardonable sin wouldn't be troubled by it, having moved beyond conviction. A tender heart that fears having committed this sin demonstrates the spiritual sensitivity that makes this sin impossible.

Key Bible Verses:

- "Anyone who speaks a word against the Son of Man will be forgiven, but anyone who speaks against the Holy Spirit will not be forgiven, either in this age or in the age to come." (Matthew 12:32)

- "If we confess our sins, he is faithful and just and will forgive us our sins and purify us from all unrighteousness." (1 John 1:9)

- "Everyone who calls on the name of the Lord will be saved." (Romans 10:13)

Question 40: Can Christians lose their salvation?

This question has long been debated among sincere believers. Scripture emphasizes God's faithfulness in preserving His people and our responsibility to persevere in faith. Let's contemplate the biblical evidence.

Many passages strongly affirm the security of the believer:

- Jesus says, "I give them eternal life, and they shall never perish; no one will snatch them out of my hand" (John 10:28)

- Paul declares, "He who began a good work in you will carry it on to completion" (Philippians 1:6)

- Romans 8:38-39 assures us that nothing can separate us from God's love

- Believers are sealed with the Holy Spirit as a guarantee (Ephesians 1:13-14)

Other passages warn against falling away:

- Hebrews 6:4-6 cautions about those who "fall away" after experiencing spiritual blessings

- Jesus speaks of branches that don't bear fruit being cut off (John 15:2)

- Paul urges believers to "continue in his kindness. Otherwise, you also will be cut off" (Romans 11:22)

How do we reconcile these? Many evangelical scholars suggest that genuine salvation, rooted in God's sovereign election and grace, cannot be lost. Those who permanently turn away demonstrate they were never truly regenerated, despite appearances (1 John 2:19).

Rather than creating anxiety, this teaching should inspire both confidence and vigilance. We trust in God's power to keep us while taking seriously the call to "work out your salvation with fear and trembling" (Philippians 2:12). Genuine faith perseveres to the end—not earning salvation but demonstrating its reality.

Key Bible Verses:

- "I give them eternal life, and they shall never perish; no one will snatch them out of my hand." (John 10:28)

- "They went out from us, but they did not really belong to us. For if they had belonged to us, they would have remained with us; but their going showed that none of them belonged to us." (1 John 2:19)
- "To him who is able to keep you from stumbling and to present you before his glorious presence without fault and with great joy." (Jude 24)

Section 5: The Bible and Its Authority

Question 41: What is the Bible?

The Bible is the divinely inspired collection of 66 books God has given as His authoritative revelation to humanity. It is divided into the Old Testament (39 books) and the New Testament (27 books), written over approximately 1,500 years by around 40 human authors from diverse backgrounds, including shepherds, kings, fishermen, doctors, tax collectors, and more.

The Old Testament records God's creation of the world, the fall of humanity, God's covenant with Israel, and the anticipation of a coming Messiah. The New Testament reveals Jesus as the Messiah, documents the birth of the Church, and provides instruction for Christian living.

Though written by human authors, the Bible is ultimately God's Word. Second Timothy 3:16 states, "All Scripture is God-breathed"—meaning God divinely inspired every word. The human writers weren't merely taking dictation, but God guided their thoughts and words while respecting their personalities, styles, and contexts.

The Bible is unlike any other book in its:

- Unity (remarkable consistency despite diverse authors and centuries of writing)
- Historical accuracy (confirmed by archaeology and external sources)
- Fulfilled prophecy (hundreds of specific predictions later fulfilled)
- Life-changing power (transforming individuals and societies)
- Preservation (surviving centuries of attempts to destroy it)

Scripture isn't merely a collection of human religious reflections but God's authoritative self-revelation, showing who He is, what He has done, and how we can know Him personally.

Key Bible Verses:

- "All Scripture is God-breathed and is useful for teaching, rebuking, correcting and training in righteousness." (2 Timothy 3:16)
- "For prophecy never had its origin in the human will, but prophets, though human, spoke from God as they were carried along by the Holy Spirit." (2 Peter 1:21)
- "The word of God is alive and active. Sharper than any double-edged sword, it penetrates even to dividing soul and spirit, joints and marrow; it judges the thoughts and attitudes of the heart." (Hebrews 4:12)

Question 42: Is the Bible really the Word of God?

This question strikes at the heart of Christian faith. If the Bible is merely a human book containing religious thoughts, it holds no more authority than any other text. But if it's truly God's Word, it carries divine authority and deserves our complete trust and obedience.

Scripture claims divine authorship. Phrases like "This is what the LORD says" appear thousands of times. Jesus treated the Old Testament as God's authoritative Word (Matthew 5:17-18) and promised divine guidance for the New Testament authors (John 16:13). Peter recognized Paul's writings as Scripture (2 Peter 3:16), showing the early church's understanding of ongoing divine revelation.

Several lines of evidence support the Bible's divine origin:

First, its remarkable unity. Despite dozens of authors writing over centuries in different languages, cultures, and continents, Scripture presents a consistent message without contradiction.

Second, its historical accuracy. Archaeological discoveries consistently confirm biblical details about people, places, and events once questioned by critics.

Third, its prophetic fulfillment. The Bible contains hundreds of specific prophecies that were later fulfilled exactly as predicted—many of which concern the Messiah, fulfilled in Jesus.

Fourth, its transformative power. Throughout history, Scripture has changed individuals and societies in ways no human book could accomplish.

Fifth, its supernatural preservation despite centuries of attempts to destroy it.

While faith is ultimately required to accept the Bible as God's Word, this faith isn't blind—it's supported by compelling evidence. As we approach Scripture humbly and honestly, its divine voice becomes increasingly apparent.

Key Bible Verses:

- "All Scripture is God-breathed and is useful for teaching, rebuking, correcting and training in righteousness." (2 Timothy 3:16)

- "Above all, you must understand that no prophecy of Scripture came about by the prophet's own interpretation of things. For prophecy never had its origin in the human will, but prophets, though human, spoke from God as they were carried along by the Holy Spirit." (2 Peter 1:20-21)

- "Heaven and earth will pass away, but my words will never pass away." (Matthew 24:35)

Question 43: Who wrote the Bible?

The Bible is unlike any other book in history. It has a unique dual authorship: God is its ultimate Author, yet He chose to communicate His Word through human writers over approximately 1,500 years.

On the divine side, Scripture is described as *"God-breathed"* (2 Timothy 3:16). That means every word originates from God, not merely as human ideas about Him, but as His revealed truth. Second Peter 1:21 explains how this happened: *"For prophecy never had its origin in the human will, but prophets, though human, spoke from God as they were carried along by the Holy Spirit."* The Holy Spirit guided the human authors so that what they wrote was precisely what God intended—without error and full of purpose.

On the human side, God used around 40 different individuals from diverse background, including — shepherds, kings, prophets, fishermen, scholars, and physicians. These included:

- Moses, traditionally credited with writing the first five books of the Bible (Genesis through Deuteronomy).

- David and Solomon, whose psalms, proverbs, and reflections, form much of the wisdom literature.

- Prophets like Isaiah, Jeremiah, and Ezekiel, who spoke boldly on God's behalf to Israel and the nations.

- Historical leaders, such as Ezra and Nehemiah, who chronicled the return from exile.

- Gospel writers like Matthew (a tax collector), Mark (a companion of Peter), Luke (a physician), and John (a beloved disciple).

- The apostle Paul, who wrote many of the New Testament letters to early churches and Christian leaders.

God did not bypass their personalities, vocabularies, or life experiences. Instead, He worked through them. You can see David's poetic heart in the Psalms, Paul's logical reasoning in his epistles, and Luke's medical precision in his Gospel and the Acts of the Apostles. This rich diversity adds beauty and depth to Scripture, even as its unified message remains consistent from the beginning of Genesis to the end of Revelation.

Key Bible Verses:

- *"All Scripture is God-breathed and is useful for teaching, rebuking, correcting and training in righteousness."* (2 Timothy 3:16)

- *"Prophets, though human, spoke from God as they were carried along by the Holy Spirit."* (2 Peter 1:21)

- *"The word of the Lord came to..."* (a phrase used frequently by prophets, affirming divine origin)

Question 44: How do we know the Bible hasn't been changed?

With thousands of years between the original biblical writings and our modern Bibles, it's reasonable to wonder if the text has been substantially altered or corrupted over time. The evidence, however, strongly supports the Bible's remarkable preservation.

For the Old Testament, the discovery of the Dead Sea Scrolls in 1947 provided extraordinary confirmation of textual accuracy. These manuscripts, dating from around 250 BC to 68 AD, included biblical texts approximately 1,000 years older than the previously available Hebrew manuscripts. They showed astonishing consistency compared to medieval texts, demonstrating the meticulous care with which Jewish scribes preserved Scripture.

For the New Testament, we possess an unprecedented wealth of manuscript evidence:

- Over 5,800 Greek manuscripts, some dating to within decades of the original writings
- More than 10,000 Latin manuscripts and thousands in other early languages
- Quotations from early church writers so extensive that nearly the entire New Testament could be reconstructed from them alone

This abundant evidence allows scholars to compare manuscripts, identify variations, and establish with over 99% certainty what the original documents said. The few remaining textual questions do not affect any central doctrine or teaching.

Modern translations are based on the best manuscript evidence, with teams of scholars carefully evaluating the ancient texts. While translation philosophies differ (from more literal to more dynamic), principal evangelical translations faithfully represent the original meaning.

God has preserved His Word throughout history, ensuring that we can trust today's Bible to reflect accurately what the original authors wrote under divine inspiration.

Key Bible Verses:

- "The grass withers and the flowers fall, but the word of our God endures forever." (Isaiah 40:8)
- "Heaven and earth will pass away, but my words will never pass away." (Matthew 24:35)
- "Your word, LORD, is eternal; it stands firm in the heavens." (Psalm 119:89)

Question 45: What is the purpose of the Bible?

God has given us Scripture to increase our knowledge and transform our lives. Understanding the Bible's purposes helps us approach it with the right expectations and an open mind to its work in us.

The primary purpose of Scripture is to reveal God Himself—His character works and will. While creation shows God's power and divine nature (Romans 1:20), the Bible provides a much fuller picture of God and what He desires for humanity. Scripture teaches us about God's holiness, love, justice, mercy, and faithfulness.

The Bible also points us to Jesus Christ. Jesus tells the religious leaders, "These are the very Scriptures that testify about me" (John 5:39). From Genesis to Revelation, the Bible unfolds God's plan of redemption through Christ. The Gospels specifically record Jesus' life, teachings, death, and resurrection so "that you may believe that Jesus is the Messiah, the Son of God and that by believing you may have life in his name" (John 20:31).

Additionally, Scripture equips believers for godly living. As 2 Timothy 3:16-17 explains, it teaches truth, corrects error, rebukes sin, and trains in righteousness "so that the servant of God may be thoroughly equipped for every good work." It provides wisdom for daily decisions, comfort in suffering, and guidance for relationships.

Scripture also builds faith, offers hope, and strengthens our relationship with God. Romans 15:4 states, "Everything that was written in the past was written to teach us so that through the endurance taught in the Scriptures and the encouragement they provide, we might have hope."

When we approach the Bible to understand these purposes, we read not just for information but for transformation—allowing God's Word to shape our thinking, redirect our desires, and guide our actions.

Key Bible Verses:

- "All Scripture is God-breathed and is useful for teaching, rebuking, correcting and training in righteousness, so that the servant of God may be thoroughly equipped for every good work." (2 Timothy 3:16-17)

- "These are written that you may believe that Jesus is the Messiah, the Son of God and that by believing you may have life in his name." (John 20:31)

- "Your word is a lamp for my feet, a light on my path." (Psalm 119:105)

Question 46: Is the Bible historically reliable?

Critical scholars have sometimes portrayed the Bible as historically unreliable, filled with myths and legends rather than accurate accounts. However, archaeological discoveries and historical research increasingly confirm Scripture's historical trustworthiness.

Numerous archaeological findings have verified biblical details once questioned by critics:

- The existence of Hittite civilization, once doubted, was confirmed by extensive archaeological discoveries

- The Pool of Bethesda (John 5:2) was uncovered in Jerusalem with the five porticoes described in Scripture

- Pontius Pilate's name was found inscribed on a stone in Caesarea, confirming the Gospel accounts

- The ruins of Jericho show evidence of walls that fell outward, consistent with the biblical account

- Discoveries in Nineveh confirmed details about Assyrian kings mentioned in the Bible

Historical and cultural details in the Gospels reflect a remarkable accuracy in knowledge of first-century Palestine, including customs, geography, politics, and religious practices. The Gospel of Luke has been praised even by skeptical scholars for its historical accuracy, as it mentions specific officials, places, and events that align with other historical sources.

The New Testament documents were written within the lifetime of eyewitnesses who could have disputed inaccurate accounts. The apostle Paul appeals to this fact when writing about Jesus' resurrection appearances (1 Corinthians 15:6).

While the Bible's purpose isn't primarily to provide historical documentation, its historical claims have repeatedly withstood scrutiny. We can confidently trust that Scripture records real events in real places involving real people, a faith grounded in historical reality, not mythological imagination.

Key Bible Verses:

- "Many have undertaken to draw up an account of the things that have been fulfilled among us, just as they were handed down to us by those who from the first were eyewitnesses and servants of the word. With this in mind, since I myself have carefully investigated everything from the beginning, I too decided to write an orderly account for you, most excellent Theophilus, so that you may know the certainty of the things you have been taught." (Luke 1:1-4)

- "For we did not follow cleverly devised stories when we told you about the coming of our Lord Jesus Christ in power, but we were eyewitnesses of his majesty." (2 Peter 1:16)

- "The third day he rose again from the dead...he appeared to more than five hundred of the brothers and sisters at the same time, most of whom are still living." (1 Corinthians 15:4-6)

Question 47: How should I read and study the Bible?

The Bible is God's living Word, able to transform our hearts and minds. But many find Bible reading challenging or confusing. Here are practical principles for meaningful Bible study.

First, approach Scripture prayerfully. Ask God to guide your understanding and open your heart to His truth. Psalm 119:18 models this attitude: "Open my eyes that I may see wonderful things in your law." The same Holy Spirit who inspired Scripture helps us understand it (John 16:13).

Second, read systematically rather than randomly. While occasional verse-by-verse reading has value, regularly working through entire books provides context and deeper understanding. For beginners, consider starting with the Gospel of John, then Romans or Ephesians.

Third, observe before interpreting. Ask: What does the passage say? Who wrote it, to whom, and why? What literary genre is it (history, poetry, letters, etc.)? Understanding these basics helps prevent misinterpretation.

Fourth, interpret Scripture with Scripture. Since the Bible doesn't contradict itself, unclear passages should be understood considering clearer ones. Cross references and study Bibles can help identify related passages.

Fifth, focus on application, not just information. James 1:22 warns against being hearers only and not doers of the Word. Ask: How does this passage challenge my thinking or behaviour? What action should I take in response?

Helpful resources include study Bibles, concordances, commentaries, and Bible study guides. Many are available online or as apps. Consider joining a small group Bible study for accountability and diverse perspectives.

Key Bible Verses:

- "Do your best to present yourself to God as one approved, a worker who does not need to be ashamed and who correctly handles the word of truth." (2 Timothy 2:15)

- "For the word of God is alive and active. Sharper than any double-edged sword, it penetrates even to dividing soul and spirit, joints and marrow; it judges the thoughts and attitudes of the heart." (Hebrews 4:12)

- "All Scripture is God-breathed and is useful for teaching, rebuking, correcting and training in righteousness." (2 Timothy 3:16)

Question 48: Can the Bible be trusted in today's world?

In our rapidly changing, scientifically advanced society, many wonder if an ancient book like the Bible remains relevant and trustworthy. This question deserves honest consideration.

First, although written long ago, the Bible addresses timeless human needs and questions. The fundamental issues we face—meaning, identity, morality, relationships, suffering, death—haven't changed. Modern technology may transform how we live, but it doesn't change who we are. The Bible speaks to our unchanging human condition with enduring wisdom.

Second, biblical values have repeatedly proven beneficial for individuals and societies. Principles such as human dignity, compassion for the vulnerable, forgiveness, integrity, and self-sacrifice all foster human flourishing in any era. Many modern ethical frameworks, including human rights concepts, have roots in biblical teachings.

Third, where Scripture addresses matter touching science or history, careful interpretation consistently matches established facts. The Bible wasn't written as a scientific textbook, but when properly understood, it doesn't contradict genuine scientific discoveries. Many leading scientists throughout history and today have found no conflict between their scientific work and their faith in the Bible.

Fourth, the Bible's transformative power continues in countless lives across cultures and generations. Its ability to bring people hope, healing, and purpose in diverse circumstances testifies to its ongoing relevance and power.

While understanding Scripture requires careful interpretation considering historical context and literary genre, its core message and principles remain trustworthy guides for today's complex world.

Key Bible Verses:

- "The grass withers and the flowers fall, but the word of our God endures forever." (Isaiah 40:8)

- "All Scripture is God-breathed and is useful for teaching, rebuking, correcting and training in righteousness." (2 Timothy 3:16)

- "Jesus Christ is the same yesterday and today and forever." (Hebrews 13:8)

Question 49: How was the Bible put together?

The Bible didn't drop from heaven as a completed book. Its formation was a historical process guided by God's providence, resulting in the collection of 66 books today.

The Old Testament canon, a recognized list of authoritative books, developed gradually among the Jewish people. By Jesus' time, the three divisions mentioned in Luke 24:44—the Law, the Prophets, and the Writings (Psalms)—were established mainly. Jesus and the apostles treated these Hebrew Scriptures as divinely authoritative.

The New Testament canon formed over the first few centuries of church history. The process wasn't arbitrary but recognized writings that:

- Had apostolic authority (written by apostles or their close associates)
- Were consistent with established Christian teaching
- Had been accepted and used widely in churches throughout the known world
- Demonstrated internal evidence of divine inspiration

By about AD 367, when Athanasius listed the 27 books of our New Testament, the canon was essentially settled, though formal church councils later confirmed what was already widely accepted.

It's important to note that these councils didn't create the canon but rather recognized which books had already demonstrated their divine authority through their impact on the church. God guided this process to ensure His intended revelation would be preserved.

The Bible's remarkable journey from scattered manuscripts to a unified canon demonstrates God's faithfulness in preserving His Word for all generations.

Key Bible Verses:

- "But these are written that you may believe that Jesus is the Messiah, the Son of God and that by believing you may have life in his name." (John 20:31)
- "Bear in mind that our Lord's patience means salvation, just as our dear brother Paul also wrote you with the wisdom that God gave him... His letters contain some things that are hard to understand, which ignorant and unstable people distort, as they do the other Scriptures." (2 Peter 3:15-16)
- "I warn everyone who hears the words of the prophecy of this scroll: If anyone adds anything to them, God will add to that person the plagues described in this scroll. And if anyone takes words away from this scroll of prophecy, God will take away from that person any share in the tree of life and in the Holy City." (Revelation 22:18-19)

Question 50: Why are there different Bible translations?

With dozens of English Bible translations available, many wonder which is the best or most accurate. Understanding why multiple translations exist helps answer this question.

Initially, the Bible was written in Hebrew, Aramaic (For the Old Testament), and Greek (for the New Testament). Since most people can't read these ancient languages, translation is necessary. But translation isn't a simple word-for-word substitution—languages differ in vocabulary, grammar, idioms, and cultural contexts.

Different translations reflect different approaches to this challenge:

- Formal equivalence (literal) translations like the ESV, NASB, and KJV prioritize word-for-word correspondence where possible
- Dynamic equivalence translations like the NIV and NLT aim for thought-for-thought accuracy, often sacrificing literal wording for clarity
- Paraphrases like The Message prioritize contemporary expression of meaning over literal accuracy

None of these approaches is inherently superior - they serve a different purpose. Formal equivalence translations work well for detailed study, while dynamic equivalence translations offer excellent readability and clarity, especially for new readers.

Translations also differ in the manuscript traditions they follow, the reading level they target, and whether they use gender-inclusive language for generic terms.

Rather than seeing these differences as problematic, we can view multiple translations as a blessing, helping us grasp the whole meaning of Scripture through different linguistic lenses. Many serious Bible students use several translations, comparing them to a deeper understanding.

Key Bible Verses:

- "Until I come, devote yourself to the public reading of Scripture, to preaching and to teaching." (1 Timothy 4:13)
- "Let the word of Christ dwell in you richly." (Colossians 3:16)
- "Do your best to present yourself to God as one approved, a worker who does not need to be ashamed and who correctly handles the word of truth." (2 Timothy 2:15)

Section 6: Christian Living and Ethics

Question 51: What does it mean to live the Christian life?

The Christian life is not primarily about following rules, but about a relationship with God through Jesus Christ that transforms the way we live. It begins with salvation by grace through faith but continues as a lifelong journey of growth and discipleship.

At its heart, the Christian life is about following Jesus—walking as He walked (1 John 2:6). This means:

- Loving God wholeheartedly and others sacrificially (Matthew 22:37-39)
- Becoming more like Christ in character and priorities (Romans 8:29)
- Serving others with our gifts and resources (1 Peter 4:10)
- Sharing the good news with those who don't know Jesus (Matthew 28:19-20)

This life is empowered by the Holy Spirit, not by our strength. As Galatians 2:20 expresses, "I have been crucified with Christ and I no longer live, but Christ lives in me." The Christian surrenders control to Christ, allowing His life to flow through them.

The Christian life balances several key elements:

- Personal devotion (prayer, Bible study, worship)
- Community involvement (church participation, fellowship, service)
- Public witness (living distinctly, sharing faith, showing compassion)
- Ongoing growth (continual repentance, learning, and transformation)

While not perfect or free from struggles, the genuine Christian life should display increasing freedom from sin's dominion and growing evidence of the Spirit's fruit (Galatians 5:22-23). It's a journey of becoming more authentically human as we're restored to God's original design.

Key Bible Verses:

- "I have been crucified with Christ and I no longer live, but Christ lives in me. The life I now live in the body, I live by faith in the Son of God, who loved me and gave himself for me." (Galatians 2:20)
- "Therefore, I urge you, brothers and sisters, in view of God's mercy, to offer your bodies as a living sacrifice, holy and pleasing to God—this is your true and proper worship." (Romans 12:1)
- "Whoever claims to live in him must live as Jesus did." (1 John 2:6)

Question 52: How can I grow spiritually?

Spiritual growth is the process of becoming more like Jesus Christ in our character, values, and priorities. Unlike physical growth, which happens naturally with proper nourishment, spiritual growth requires both God's grace and our intentional participation.

Scripture uses various metaphors for spiritual , such as rowth, such as a plant growing, a building being constructed, and a child maturing. All suggest a gradual process that requires time and care. Here are key elements for healthy spiritual growth:

Scripture engagement is foundational. Through God's Word, we learn His truth and align our thoughts with His (Romans 12:2). This means not just reading, but also studying, memorizing, meditating on, and applying Scripture.

Prayer connects us directly with God. Through regular, honest conversation with Him, we develop intimacy and learn dependence. Prayer includes adoration, confession, thanksgiving, and supplication (1 Thessalonians 5:17).

Worship, both corporate and private, focuses our hearts on God's worth and realigns our priorities. When we magnify God's greatness, our problems and self-focus diminish (Psalm 95:1-7).

Christian community provides accountability, encouragement, and opportunities to serve and be served. We aren't meant to grow alone but as part of Christ's body (Hebrews 10:24-25).

Obedience to God's commands is essential. Jesus said if we love Him, we will obey His commands (John 14:15). Spiritual knowledge without application leads to self-deception (James 1:22).

Even difficulties contribute to growth when we respond in faith. James 1:2-4 teaches that trials develop perseverance and maturity. God often uses challenges to deepen our dependence on Him.

Remember that growth is God's work in partnership with our cooperation. He provides the power; we make the choices to yield to Him daily.

Key Bible Verses:

- "Grow in the grace and knowledge of our Lord and Savior Jesus Christ." (2 Peter 3:18)
- "Do not conform to the pattern of this world, but be transformed by the renewing of your mind." (Romans 12:2)
- "Let us consider how we may spur one another on toward love and good deeds, not giving up meeting together." (Hebrews 10:24-25)

Question 53: Why is church important for Christians?

In an age of online sermons and individualistic spirituality, many wonder if regular church attendance is essential. Scripture, however, presents the church not as an optional add-on but as essential to Christian life.

The church is not primarily a building or institution but the community of believers—the "body of Christ" (1 Corinthians 12:27). When you became a Christian, you were incorporated into this body and given a specific function within it. Just as a physical body part cannot thrive in isolation, Christians need connection to the larger body.

Church participation provides several vital benefits:

Biblical teaching and accountability help us grow in our understanding and application of God's Word. Left to ourselves, we tend to interpret Scripture according to our preferences rather than submitting to its authority (2 Timothy 4:3-4).

Fellowship with other believers provides encouragement, support, and meaningful opportunities to live out the "one another" commands found throughout the New Testament—such as love one another, serve one another, and bear one another's burdens.

Corporate worship allows us to express devotion to God alongside others, creating a powerful testimony to His worth. Throughout Scripture, God's people are called to worship Him together, not just individually.

Ministry opportunities within the church help us discover and use our spiritual gifts. Each believer has received gifts "for the common good" (1 Corinthians 12:7), and these gifts are meant to be exercised within the context of the church body.

While gathering with other Christians doesn't require elaborate buildings or formal structures, Scripture explicitly warns against "giving up meeting together" (Hebrews 10:25). Regular participation in a local church is not just about what we receive, but also about what we contribute to Christ's body.

Key Bible Verses:

- "Let us not give up meeting together, as some are in the habit of doing, but let us encourage one another—and all the more as you see the Day approaching." (Hebrews 10:25)

- "Now you are the body of Christ, and each one of you is a part of it." (1 Corinthians 12:27)

- "They devoted themselves to the apostles' teaching and to fellowship, to the breaking of bread and to prayer." (Acts 2:42)

Question 54: What is baptism, and why is it important?

Baptism is one of the two ordinances or sacraments that Jesus established for His church, along with the Lord's Supper. It's a public ceremony where a believer is immersed in or sprinkled with water, symbolizing their identification with Christ's death, burial, and resurrection.

Jesus commands His followers to "go and make disciples of all nations, baptizing them in the name of the Father and of the Son and of the Holy Spirit" (Matthew 28:19). He Himself was baptized at the beginning of His ministry, not because He needed repentance but to "fulfill all righteousness" (Matthew 3:15) and identify with those He came to save.

Baptism serves several important purposes:

It's a public declaration of faith in Christ. Through baptism, believers openly identify themselves with Jesus and His church, declaring that they've died to their old life and been raised to new life in Him.

It symbolizes spiritual cleansing. The water represents the washing away of sin through Christ's sacrificial death (Acts 22:16).

It pictures union with Christ in His death, burial, and resurrection. Romans 6:3-4 explains that when we are baptized, we are symbolically buried with Christ and raised to live a new life.

It marks incorporation into Christ's body, the church. In 1 Corinthians 12:13, Paul writes that "we were all baptized by one Spirit so as to form one body."

Christians differ on several aspects of baptism, including the proper mode (immersion, pouring, or sprinkling), the appropriate age (infant or adult baptism), and whether it conveys grace or merely symbolizes it. However, most agree that baptism itself doesn't save us—salvation comes through faith in Christ alone (Ephesians 2:8-9).

If you've trusted Christ but haven't been baptized, consider taking this step of obedience and public identification with Him.

Key Bible Verses:

- "We were therefore buried with him through baptism into death so that, just as Christ was raised from the dead through the glory of the Father, we too may live a new life." (Romans 6:4)

- "Repent and be baptized, every one of you, in the name of Jesus Christ for the forgiveness of your sins." (Acts 2:38)

- "Whoever believes and is baptized will be saved, but whoever does not believe will be condemned." (Mark 16:16)

Question 55: What is communion (the Lord's Supper)?

Communion, also known as the Lord's Supper or Eucharist, is a sacred meal instituted by Jesus on the night before his crucifixion. Along with baptism, it's one of the two ordinances that Jesus established for His church to observe.

During the Last Supper with his disciples, Jesus took bread, gave thanks, broke it, and says, "This is my body, which is given for you; do this in remembrance of me." Then He took the cup, saying, "This cup is the new covenant in my blood, which is poured out for you" (Luke 22:19-20). These simple elements—bread or wine or juice—represent Christ's body broken and blood shed for our salvation.

Communion serves several significant purposes:

It commemorates Christ's sacrifice. Jesus instructed, "Do this in remembrance of me" (1 Corinthians 11:24-25). The bread and cup help us recall the tremendous price Jesus paid for our redemption.

It proclaims Christ's death. Paul writes, "For whenever you eat this bread and drink this cup, you proclaim the Lord's death until he comes" (1 Corinthians 11:26). Each celebration testifies to Christ's atoning work.

It fosters fellowship with Christ and His body. Sharing this meal together expresses our union with Christ and with one another as His people (1 Corinthians 10:16-17).

It anticipates Christ's return. The Lord's Supper looks not only backward to Christ's death but also forward to His coming, when we'll feast with Him in His kingdom (Matthew 26:29).

Scripture teaches that we should participate in communion with proper reverence and self-examination, discerning the significance of Christ's body (1 Corinthians 11:27-29). This doesn't mean we must be perfect to participate, but that we should approach with sincere hearts, confessing our known sins and receiving God's grace.

Christian traditions differ on how frequently communion should be observed, who may participate, and the exact meaning of the elements. However, all agree that this simple meal holds profound spiritual significance for believers.

Key Bible Verses:

- "For whenever you eat this bread and drink this cup, you proclaim the Lord's death until he comes." (1 Corinthians 11:26)
- "The Lord Jesus, on the night he was betrayed, took bread, and when he had given thanks, he broke it and said, 'This is my body, which is for you; do this in remembrance of me.'" (1 Corinthians 11:23-24)
- "Is not the cup of thanksgiving for which we give thanks a participation in the blood of Christ? And is not the bread that we break a participation in the body of Christ?" (1 Corinthians 10:16)

Question 56: How should Christians handle money?

Money plays a significant role in our lives, and Jesus spoke about it more frequently than he did about heaven, hell, or prayer. How we handle our finances reflects and influences our spiritual condition.

The foundational principle is that God owns everything. Psalm 24:1 declares, "The earth is the LORD's, and everything in it." We are stewards, not owners, entrusted with resources to manage according to God's purposes. This perspective transforms our approach to money.

From this foundation flow several key principles:

Work diligently to provide for yourself and others. Scripture commends honest labor (Ephesians 4:28) and warns against laziness (Proverbs 6:6-11). Work isn't just about earning money but about glorifying God and serving others.

Live within your means. The Bible consistently warns against the dangers of debt (Proverbs 22:7) and encourages contentment rather than always wanting more (1 Timothy 6:6-8).

Save wisely. Prudent planning for the future reflects good stewardship (Proverbs 21:20); however, we must avoid hoarding wealth or finding security in it, instead trusting in God.

Give generously. God loves cheerful giving (2 Corinthians 9:7), and generosity is a tangible expression of our trust in Him and love for others. Scripture teaches proportional giving—those with more should give more.

Use money for eternal impact. Jesus advised storing up "treasures in heaven" rather than on earth (Matthew 6:19-21). This means investing in God's kingdom—supporting church ministry, missions, and helping those in need.

Guard against materialism. Jesus warned that we cannot serve both God and money (Matthew 6:24). Cultivate gratitude for what you have rather than craving what you don't.

Remember that financial decisions are spiritual decisions. How we earn, spend, save, and give reflects and shapes our hearts. As Jesus says, "Where your treasure is, there your heart will be also" (Matthew 6:21).

Key Bible Verses:

- "Honor the LORD with your wealth, with the firstfruits of all your crops." (Proverbs 3:9)

- "Each of you should give what you have decided in your heart to give, not reluctantly or under compulsion, for God loves a cheerful giver." (2 Corinthians 9:7)

- "For the love of money is a root of all kinds of evil. Some people, eager for money, have wandered from the faith and pierced themselves with many griefs." (1 Timothy 6:10)

Question 57: What is tithing, and is it required?

Tithing—giving a tenth of one's income to God—was an explicit requirement under the Old Testament law. Malachi 3:10 instructed, "Bring the whole tithe into the storehouse." But many Christians wonder if this practice still applies under the new covenant of grace.

In the Old Testament, Israel's tithes supported the Levites, who had no land inheritance, provided for temple maintenance, and cared for the poor. This system functioned as both religious giving and a form of taxation for the theocratic nation.

Jesus affirmed the practice of tithing, while emphasizing that it shouldn't replace more critical matters, such as justice, mercy, and faithfulness (Matthew 23:23). However, the New Testament does not explicitly command Christians to tithe. Instead, it offers principles for giving:

Give regularly. Paul instructed believers to set aside money "on the first day of every week" (1 Corinthians 16:2), establishing a pattern of consistent giving.

Give proportionally. The Old Testament tithe and Paul's instruction to set aside money "in keeping with your income" (1 Corinthians 16:2) suggest giving should be proportionate to what we receive.

Give generously. Paul praised the Macedonian churches who gave "as much as they were able, and even beyond their ability" (2 Corinthians 8:3).

Give cheerfully. "God loves a cheerful giver" (2 Corinthians 9:7), not one who gives reluctantly or under compulsion.

Many Christians find the tithe (10%) a helpful starting point for giving, though the New Testament emphasis is more on the heart than a specific percentage. Those with less might begin with a smaller proportion, while those with abundance might give substantially more than a tenth.

Whether or not we consider tithing obligatory, the principle remains that generous, sacrificial giving is a vital part of Christian discipleship—reflecting God's generosity to us and our trust in His provision.

Key Bible Verses:

- "Bring the whole tithe into the storehouse, that there may be food in my house. Test me in this," says the LORD Almighty, "and see if I will not throw open the floodgates of heaven and pour out so much blessing that there will not be room enough to store it." (Malachi 3:10)

- "Each of you should give what you have decided in your heart to give, not reluctantly or under compulsion, for God loves a cheerful giver." (2 Corinthians 9:7)

- "Remember this: Whoever sows sparingly will also reap sparingly, and whoever sows generously will also reap generously." (2 Corinthians 9:6)

Question 58: How should Christians make decisions?

We face countless decisions each day—from routine choices to life-altering ones, such as career moves, marriage, or major relocations. While Scripture doesn't offer specific answers for every situation, it provides timeless principles for making decisions that honor God.

The foundation is seeking God's will rather than just our preferences. As Jesus prayed, "Not my will, but yours be done" (Luke 22:42). This requires humility and surrender, acknowledging that God's perspective exceeds our limited understanding.

With this attitude, several biblical guidelines can help us navigate decisions:

Scripture provides boundaries and principles. God's written Word reveals His character and commands, establishing clear parameters. Some choices are immediately eliminated because they contradict biblical teachings (such as dishonesty or sexual immorality).

Prayer invites God's guidance. James 1:5 promises, "If any of you lacks wisdom, you should ask God, who gives generously to all without finding fault, and it will be given to you." Bring your decisions before God, asking for clarity and direction.

Wise counsel offers perspective. Proverbs 15:22 states, "Plans fail for lack of counsel, but with many advisers they succeed." Seek input from mature believers who know Scripture and care about your spiritual well-being.

Inner peace often confirms God's leading. Colossians 3:15 instructs, "Let the peace of Christ rule in your hearts." A decision aligning with God's will typically bring peace, even if it involves challenges.

Circumstances may indicate God's direction. While not infallible, open and closed doors can provide guidance when aligned with other factors. God sometimes uses timing, opportunities, or constraints to direct our paths.

Consider creating a list of pros and cons for complex decisions, evaluated through the lens of Scripture and godly wisdom. Remember that God rarely reveals His entire plan at once—He often guides us one step at a time as we walk by faith.

Even when we seek to honour God, we sometimes make mistakes. The good news is that God is sovereign over our decisions and can redeem even our errors when we remain committed to Him.

Key Bible Verses:

- "Trust in the LORD with all your heart and lean not on your own understanding; in all your ways submit to him, and he will make your paths straight." (Proverbs 3:5-6)

- "If any of you lacks wisdom, you should ask God, who gives generously to all without finding fault, and it will be given to you." (James 1:5)

- "For we are God's handiwork, created in Christ Jesus to do good works, which God prepared in advance for us to do." (Ephesians 2:10)

Question 59: What does it mean to be holy?

Holiness can seem intimidating—conjuring images of stern-faced ascetics or impossible moral perfection. But biblical holiness is more profound and attainable than these misconceptions suggest.

At its core, holiness means being "set apart" for God—consecrated for His purposes and increasingly reflecting His character. The command to "be holy, because I am holy" (1 Peter 1:16) invites us to share in God's nature.

Holiness has both positional and practical dimensions. Positionally, believers are already "holy" (set apart) through Christ's work—"you are a chosen people, a royal priesthood, a holy nation" (1 Peter 2:9). Practically, we're called to grow in holiness through ongoing transformation—"purify ourselves from everything that contaminates body and spirit, perfecting holiness out of reverence for God" (2 Corinthians 7:1).

This practical holiness involves:

Separation from sin. Holiness means saying "no" increasingly to what dishonors God. This isn't just about avoiding external vices and addressing heart attitudes like pride, bitterness, and selfishness.

Dedication to God. Holiness is as much about what we embrace as what we avoid—consecrating our lives to God's purposes. Romans 12:1 describes offering our bodies as "a living sacrifice, holy and pleasing to God."

Transformation into Christ's likeness. Holiness isn't achieved through willpower but through surrender to the Holy Spirit's work, which gradually conforms us to Christ's image (2 Corinthians 3:18).

Importantly, holiness isn't about earning God's approval but responding to the love and grace He has already shown us. It's not primarily about rule-keeping but about relationships—loving what God loves and hating what He hates.

While perfect holiness awaits Christ's return (1 John 3:2-3), every believer can grow in practical holiness by depending on the Spirit, engaging with Scripture, and participating in the Christian community.

Key Bible Verses:

- "Just as he who called you is holy, so be holy in all you do; for it is written: 'Be holy, because I am holy.'" (1 Peter 1:15-16)

- "It is God's will that you should be sanctified... For God did not call us to be impure, but to live a holy life." (1 Thessalonians 4:3, 7)

- "Make every effort to live in peace with everyone and to be holy; without holiness no one will see the Lord." (Hebrews 12:14)

Question 60: What is the role of the Ten Commandments today?

The Ten Commandments, given to Moses by God at Mount Sinai (Exodus 20:1-17), have shaped moral understanding for centuries. But Christians often wonder about their relevance today, especially since Scripture indicates that we are "not under the law, but under grace" (Romans 6:14).

The Ten Commandments were part of God's covenant with the Israelites. While this specific covenant no longer applies to believers in Christ, the moral principles behind the commandments reflect God's unchanging character and standards for human behaviour.

Jesus didn't abolish the commandments but fulfilled them (Matthew 5:17) and summarized them as loving God completely and loving your neighbour as yourself (Matthew 22:37-40). He pointed to the commandments (Mark 10:17-19) when asked about eternal life, showing their enduring moral relevance.

For Christians today, the Ten Commandments serve several essential functions:

They reveal God's moral character—Holiness, justice, and goodness. The commandments aren't arbitrary rules but reflect who God is.

They expose our sinfulness and need for Christ. Like a mirror showing dirt on our faces, the law reveals where we fall short (Romans 3:20), driving us to depend on Christ's righteousness rather than our own.

They provide moral guidance. While not comprehensive, the commandments address fundamental aspects of our relationship with God (commands 1-4) and others (commands 5-10), offering wisdom for godly living.

They're fulfilled through love. Paul wrote, "The entire law is fulfilled in keeping this one command: 'Love your neighbour as yourself'" (Galatians 5:14). The Spirit enables us to fulfill the law's righteous requirements through Christ-centred love.

Christians obey these principles not to earn salvation but out of love for Christ and a desire to honor Him. We approach the commandments not as a burden but as a description of the life God designed us to enjoy.

Key Bible Verses:

- "If you love me, keep my commands." (John 14:15)

- "Do we, then, nullify the law by this faith? Not at all! Rather, we uphold the law." (Romans 3:31)

- "Love does not harm a neighbour. Therefore love is the fulfillment of the law." (Romans 13:10)

Section 7: Church and Community

61. What is the Church, and why is it important?

The Church is not a building or a denomination—it is the spiritual family of all believers in Jesus Christ. The Bible calls it the "body of Christ," where every member has a purpose and function (1 Corinthians 12:27).

The Church exists to glorify God, build up believers, and reach the world with the Gospel. Acts 2:42-47 paints a beautiful picture of the early church: they gathered for teaching, fellowship, prayer, and breaking bread. They worshiped together, supported one another, and shared Christ with others.

Being part of a church helps us grow in faith. Hebrews 10:24-25 encourages us to meet regularly to spur one another on in love and good deeds. While the Church isn't perfect, it is God's chosen instrument for maturing His people and fulfilling His mission.

Key Bible Verses:

- "Now you are the body of Christ, and each one of you is a part of it." (1 Corinthians 12:27)
- "They devoted themselves to the apostles' teaching and fellowship, to the breaking of bread and to prayer." (Acts 2:42)
- "Let us not give up meeting together, as some are in the habit of doing, but let us encourage one another." (Hebrews 10:25)

62. What are the ordinances or sacraments of the Church?

Evangelical churches commonly observe two main ordinances instituted by Jesus: baptism and the Lord's Supper (communion).

Baptism is a public declaration of faith. It symbolizes dying to sin and being raised to new life in Christ (Romans 6:3-4). While it doesn't save us, it is a step of obedience that outwardly reflects inward transformation.

The Lord's Supper is a sacred reminder of Christ's death. When believers take the bread and the cup, they remember His sacrifice, examine their hearts, and proclaim His return (1 Corinthians 11:23-26).

These practices are more than rituals—they help anchor our faith in Christ's finished work and unite us with fellow believers.

Key Bible Verses:

- "Or don't you know that all of us who were baptized into Christ Jesus were baptized into his death?" (Romans 6:3)
- "For whenever you eat this bread and drink this cup, you proclaim the Lord's death until he comes." (1 Corinthians 11:26)

- "For we were all baptized by one Spirit so as to form one body." (1 Corinthians 12:13)

63. What is the role of pastors and church leaders?

Pastors and church leaders are entrusted with caring for, teaching, and overseeing the spiritual needs of the local church. They are called to equip God's people for works of service (Ephesians 4:11-13), guide them with humility, and serve as examples to the flock (1 Peter 5:2-3).

They must handle Scripture faithfully, counsel wisely, and shepherd the church with love and integrity. Their role is not about status or control—it's about servant leadership modelled after Jesus, who came "not to be served, but to serve" (Mark 10:45).

A church's health often reflects its leaders' character and faithfulness. That's why Scripture holds them to high standards (1 Timothy 3:1-13) and warns those who teach false doctrine or lead with selfish motives.

Key Bible Verses:

- "So Christ himself gave the apostles, the prophets, the evangelists, the pastors and teachers, to equip his people for works of service." (Ephesians 4:11-12)
- "Be shepherds of God's flock that is under your care, watching over them—not because you must, but because you are willing." (1 Peter 5:2)
- "Not lording it over those entrusted to you, but being examples to the flock." (1 Peter 5:3)

64. Why are there so many denominations?

Over time, differences in theology, worship style, governance, and cultural background led to the formation of denominations. While this diversity can seem divisive, many denominations hold firmly to the core truths of Christianity—such as salvation by grace through faith in Jesus and the authority of Scripture.

The Bible calls us to unity in the essentials (Ephesians 4:3-6) while allowing room for differences in non-essential matters. Despite denominational lines, we can still work together to advance God's kingdom when Christ remains at the center.

Some divisions stem from sincere biblical convictions, while others, unfortunately, reflect human pride or cultural prejudice. The solution isn't necessarily organizational unity, but a spirit of love and cooperation among all who follow Jesus, recognizing that we are part of one universal Church despite our differences.

Key Bible Verses:

- "Make every effort to keep the unity of the Spirit through the bond of peace." (Ephesians 4:3)
- "There is one body and one Spirit, just as you were called to one hope." (Ephesians 4:4)

- "I appeal to you, brothers and sisters, in the name of our Lord Jesus Christ, that all of you agree with one another in what you say and that there be no divisions among you." (1 Corinthians 1:10)

65. What is church discipline, and why does it matter?

Church discipline is a loving process of restoring a believer caught in persistent, unrepentant sin. Jesus outlined this in Matthew 18:15-17—beginning with private correction and, if needed, progressing to community involvement.

The goal is never to shame but to rescue—to help the person restore the right relationships with God and others. It also helps protect the church's testimony and encourages holiness within the body (Galatians 6:1).

Handled with grace and truth, church discipline reflects God's heart: slow to anger, abounding in love, yet committed to righteousness. When churches neglect this responsibility, they risk compromising their witness and allowing the destructive influence of sin to spread.

Key Bible Verses:

- "If your brother or sister sins, go and point out their fault, just between the two of you." (Matthew 18:15)
- "Brothers and sisters, if someone is caught in a sin, you who live by the Spirit should restore that person gently." (Galatians 6:1)
- "Warn a divisive person once, and then warn them a second time. After that, have nothing to do with them." (Titus 3:10)

66. Why is fellowship with other believers critical?

Fellowship is more than socializing—it's a spiritual connection rooted in our shared life in Christ. Acts 2:42 highlights the early church's devotion to fellowship, teaching, prayer, and the brief making of bread.

Through Christian fellowship, we find encouragement, accountability, support during trials, and joy in sharing our faith. Galatians 6:2 calls us to "carry each other's burdens," and Hebrews 10:24 urges us to "spur one another and build each other up."

Isolation weakens faith, but fellowship strengthens it. God designed us to walk together. When we withdraw from the Christian community, we become more vulnerable to discouragement, doctrinal error, and temptation. The Christian life was never meant to be lived alone.

Key Bible Verses:

- "They devoted themselves to the apostles' teaching and to fellowship." (Acts 2:42)
- "Carry each other's burdens, and in this way you will fulfill the law of Christ." (Galatians 6:2)

- "And let us consider how we may spur one another on toward love and good deeds." (Hebrews 10:24)

67. What are spiritual gifts, and how do I discover mine?

Spiritual gifts are God-given abilities, distributed by the Holy Spirit, to build up the body of Christ (1 Corinthians 12:4-11). These gifts vary—teaching, serving, encouragement, leadership, mercy, and more (Romans 12:6-8).

You can discover your gifts through prayer, studying Scripture, observing where you bear fruit, and receiving feedback from others. Serving in different areas often reveals how God has uniquely gifted you.

Every believer has a role to play, and discovering your gifts helps you serve with joy and impact. Remember that gifts are for the common good, not personal advancement. They function best within the community and should always be exercised with love (1 Corinthians 13).

Key Bible Verses:

- "There are different kinds of gifts, but the same Spirit distributes them." (1 Corinthians 12:4)
- "Each of you should use whatever gift you have received to serve others." (1 Peter 4:10)
- "We have different gifts, according to the grace given to each of us." (Romans 12:6)

68. Can a Christian worship outside a traditional church setting?

Yes. Worship is not limited to a church building. Jesus says true worshipers "will worship the Father in the Spirit and in truth" (John 4:23). You can worship through prayer, music, Scripture, or service—wherever you are.

That said, regular fellowship with other believers is essential. Whether in a traditional church, a small group, or a house gathering, connecting to a Christian community is part of God's design for your spiritual health.

The early church met both in the temple courts and in homes (Acts 2:46). What matters most is the location and the presence of biblical teaching, worship, fellowship, and outreach. Wherever believers gather in Jesus' name, He is present (Matthew 18:20).

Key Bible Verses:

- "Yet a time is coming and has now come when the true worshipers will worship the Father in the Spirit and in truth." (John 4:23)
- "Day after day, in the temple courts and from house to house, they never stopped teaching and proclaiming the good news." (Acts 5:42)
- "For where two or three gather in my name, there am I with them." (Matthew 18:20)

69. What is the mission of the Church?

The mission of the Church is to make disciples of all nations (Matthew 28:19-20). This includes evangelizing the lost, teaching God's Word, baptizing believers, and equipping people to live as faithful followers of Christ.

The Church is also called to reflect Christ's love through compassion, justice, and service. We are to be "salt and light" in a dark world (Matthew 5:13-16), pointing others to the hope found in Jesus.

This mission extends to every part of life and every corner of creation. It's lived out globally through missions and locally through acts of neighbour love. Until Christ returns, the Church continues His work of reconciling the world to God (2 Corinthians 5:18-20).

Key Bible Verses:

- "Therefore go and make disciples of all nations, baptizing them in the name of the Father and of the Son and of the Holy Spirit." (Matthew 28:19)
- "You are the light of the world. A town built on a hill cannot be hidden." (Matthew 5:14)
- "We are therefore Christ's ambassadors, as though God were making his appeal through us." (2 Corinthians 5:20)

70. What should I do if I've been hurt by the Church?

Church hurt is real—and painful. When leaders fail, or members wound us, it can shake our faith. But the brokenness of people doesn't change the beauty of Christ or His community design.

Bring your hurt to God. Seek healing through prayer, wise counsel, and, if needed, professional support. Forgive where possible, even if reconciliation isn't. Romans 12:18 says, "If it is possible, as far as it depends on you, live at peace with everyone."

Don't let hurt push you away from the Church. Let it deepen your dependence on Jesus, who will never fail you. When ready, find a healthy church community where you can heal and grow. Remember that despite its flaws, the Church remains God's family and your spiritual home.

Key Bible Verses:

- "Bear with each other and forgive one another if any of you has a grievance against someone." (Colossians 3:13)
- "If it is possible, as far as it depends on you, live at peace with everyone." (Romans 12:18)
- "The Lord is close to the brokenhearted and saves those who are crushed in spirit." (Psalm 34:18)

Section 8: Heaven and Hell

71. Is attending church necessary for salvation?

Salvation comes through grace through faith in Jesus Christ, not church attendance (Ephesians 2:8-9). However, attending church is a vital part of following Jesus.

The early believers gathered regularly for teaching, prayer, and fellowship (Acts 2:42). Hebrews 10:25 encourages us not to stop meeting together. Church participation helps us grow, encourages accountability, and equips us to serve others.

You don't go to church to be saved but because you are. Loving Jesus includes loving what He loves—and He loves His Church. While church attendance doesn't earn salvation, persistent avoidance of Christian fellowship often reveals a heart problem that should concern us.

Key Bible Verses:

- "For it is by grace you have been saved, through faith—and this is not from yourselves, it is the gift of God—not by works." (Ephesians 2:8-9)
- "Let us not give up meeting together, as some are in the habit of doing." (Hebrews 10:25)
- "They devoted themselves to the apostles' teaching and to fellowship, to the breaking of bread and to prayer." (Acts 2:42)

Question 72: What is heaven?

Heaven is often misunderstood as a vague, ethereal place where disembodied spirits float on clouds playing harps. The biblical picture is far richer and more substantial.

Scripture uses the term "heaven" in several ways. Sometimes, it refers to the sky or outer space (Genesis 1:8). Other times, it means God's dwelling place—where His presence is most directly manifest (Psalm 11:4). But when discussing the eternal destiny of believers, heaven ultimately refers to the renewed creation where God will dwell with His people forever.

The fullness of heaven comes after Christ's return and the resurrection. This "new heaven and new earth" (Revelation 21:1) will be a physical reality, not just a spiritual state. We will have resurrected bodies (Philippians 3:21) in a renewed, physical world. Far from escaping the material universe, God plans to redeem and perfect it.

Heaven will include:

Perfect relationship with God. Revelation 21:3 describes God dwelling directly with His people: "God himself will be with them and be their God." The barrier of sin that limited our intimacy with God will be gone, allowing face-to-face communion.

Reunion with other believers. Jesus spoke of people coming "from east and west" to sit at the table with Abraham, Isaac, and Jacob (Matthew 8:11), suggesting recognition and fellowship with others from diverse backgrounds.

Freedom from all suffering. God "will wipe every tear from their eyes. There will be no more death or mourning or crying or pain" (Revelation 21:4). All consequences of sin and the curse will be removed.

Meaningful activity and purpose. Contrary to the stereotype of heaven as an endless, potentially boring worship service, Scripture suggests that there is purposeful work and responsibility. Jesus speaks of ruling over cities (Luke 19:17), and Revelation describes reigning with Christ (Revelation 22:5).

While we can only glimpse heaven's glory, Jesus promised it would exceed our imagination. Our greatest joys on earth are mere shadows of the reality awaiting believers. As C.S. Lewis wrote, "All the things that have ever deeply possessed your soul have been but hints of it."

Key Bible Verses:

- "Then I saw 'a new heaven and a new earth,' for the first heaven and the first earth had passed away, and there was no longer any sea." (Revelation 21:1)
- "He will wipe every tear from their eyes. There will be no more death or mourning or crying or pain, for the old order of things has passed away." (Revelation 21:4)
- "No eye has seen, no ear has heard, no mind has conceived what God has prepared for those who love him." (1 Corinthians 2:9)

Question 73: What is hell?

Hell is one of the Bible's most challenging teachings, yet Jesus spoke about it more than almost anyone else in Scripture. Understanding this brutal reality is essential for grasping the whole biblical message.

At its core, hell is the state of permanent separation from God's presence and blessing. Scripture describes it using various images: outer darkness (Matthew 8:12), unquenchable fire (Mark 9:43), and a place of weeping and gnashing of teeth (Matthew 13:50). These likely combine literal and metaphorical elements to convey the severity of this condition.

The Bible indicates hell involves:

Conscious existence. Jesus' parable of the rich man and Lazarus (Luke 16:19-31) portrays the awareness that continue that continues after death for those separated from God.

Separation from God's presence. Paul describes it as "everlasting destruction and shut out from the presence of the Lord" (2 Thessalonians 1:9). Since all good things come from God, this separation means the absence of joy, hope, love, and all that makes life meaningful.

Justice for sin. Hell reflects God's holiness and justice. Sin against an infinitely holy God carries infinite consequences, especially when one has rejected God's offer of forgiveness in Christ.

Eternal duration. Jesus used the same word to describe both eternal life and eternal punishment (Matthew 25:46), indicating both are unending.

This teaching raises difficult questions. How could a loving God send people to hell? In reality, God doesn't "send" people there so much as to respect their choice to reject Him. C.S. Lewis observed that there are only two kinds of people in the end: those who say to God, "Thy will be done," and those to whom God says, "Thy will be done." Hell is the natural consequence of choosing life without God.

Rather than focusing on the details of hell, we should let this sobering reality increase our gratitude for salvation and our urgency in sharing the gospel. Jesus endured separation from the Father on the cross so we wouldn't have to experience eternal separation.

Key Bible Verses:

- "Then they will go away to eternal punishment, but the righteous to eternal life." (Matthew 25:46)

- "They will be punished with everlasting destruction and shut out from the presence of the Lord and from the glory of his might." (2 Thessalonians 1:9)

- "Then death and Hades were thrown into the lake of fire. The lake of fire is the second death." (Revelation 20:14)

Question 74: Will we recognize people in heaven?

The idea of reuniting with loved ones is one of the most comforting aspects of heaven for many believers. But will we recognize and know each other in the afterlife?

Scripture strongly suggests we will maintain our identities and recognize others in heaven. Several passages support this understanding:

At the Transfiguration, Moses and Elijah appeared, recognizable even though they had died centuries earlier (Matthew 17:1-3). The disciples somehow knew who these men were, suggesting identity persists beyond death.

Jesus indicated recognition when He spoke of many coming "from the east and the west" to sit at the feast with Abraham, Isaac, and Jacob in the kingdom of heaven (Matthew 8:11). This implies both recognition and relationship.

Paul expected to know the Thessalonian believers in heaven, calling them his "hope, joy, and crown" at Christ's coming (1 Thessalonians 2:19-20). This makes sense only if he would recognize them.

Paul also stated that in heaven, "I shall know fully, even as I am fully known" (1 Corinthians 13:12). This suggests enhanced, not diminished, knowledge of others.

In Jesus' parable, the rich man recognized Abraham and Lazarus in the afterlife (Luke 16:19-31), indicating consciousness and recognition continue after death.

Our resurrection bodies will be transformed, but this doesn't mean we'll lose our identity. Jesus' resurrection body was changed yet recognizable—though sometimes there was a brief delay in recognition (Luke 24:31; John 20:14-16).

The Bible indicates we'll maintain our unique identities in eternity while being freed from sin and limitation. We'll know each other more deeply than we do now—without the misconceptions, prejudices, and self-centeredness that hinder relationships on earth.

Some wonder if memories of loved ones who aren't in heaven would bring sorrow. While Scripture doesn't directly address this, we know God "will wipe every tear from their eyes" (Revelation 21:4). However, He accomplishes this, and we can trust Him to resolve such tensions as we experience His perfect joy.

Key Bible Verses:

- "After six days Jesus took with him Peter, James and John... There he was transfigured before them. His face shone like the sun, and his clothes became as white as the light. Just then there appeared before them Moses and Elijah, talking with Jesus." (Matthew 17:1-3)

- "I tell you, many will come from east and west and recline at table with Abraham, Isaac, and Jacob in the kingdom of heaven." (Matthew 8:11)

- "For now we see only a reflection as in a mirror; then we shall see face to face. Now I know in part; then I shall know fully, even as I am fully known." (1 Corinthians 13:12)

Question 75: What is the resurrection of the dead?

The resurrection of the dead is the future event when God will raise all people—believers and unbelievers—from death, reuniting their souls with bodies that are transformed. While many religious and philosophical systems teach the soul's immortality, Christianity uniquely emphasizes bodily resurrection.

Jesus' resurrection serves as both the foundation and pattern for this hope. His resurrection wasn't merely a spiritual experience or His followers' subjective impression—He was raised bodily, with a transformed yet physical body that could be touched (Luke 24:39), eat food (Luke 24:42-43), and bear the marks of crucifixion (John 20:27).

For believers, the resurrection will be glorious. Paul describes it in 1 Corinthians 15:42-44: "The body that is sown is perishable, it is raised imperishable; it is sown in dishonour, it is raised in glory; it is sown in weakness, it is raised in power; it is sown a natural body, it is raised a spiritual body." Our resurrection bodies will be free from disease, aging, and death—ideally suited for eternal life in God's presence.

Unbelievers will also be resurrected but for judgment rather than glory. Jesus says, "A time is coming when all who are in their graves will hear his voice and come out—those who have done what is good will rise to live, and those who have done what is evil will rise to be condemned" (John 5:28-29).

The resurrection is central to Christian hope. It proclaims that God values His physical creation, including our bodies. It promises the reversal of death—our final enemy (1 Corinthians 15:26).

And it guarantees that God's justice will ultimately prevail as all people stand before Him to give account.

This hope fundamentally shapes how Christian view death, suffering, and the human body. Death becomes a temporary separation rather than a final defeat. Suffering, while painful, isn't the last word. And our bodies, though currently flawed, are destined for glory—not to be despised, but cared for as temples of the Holy Spirit awaiting transformation.

Key Bible Verses:

- "For the trumpet will sound, the dead will be raised imperishable, and we will be changed." (1 Corinthians 15:52)

- "For the Lord himself will come down from heaven, with a loud command, with the voice of the archangel and with the trumpet call of God, and the dead in Christ will rise first." (1 Thessalonians 4:16)

- "Multitudes who sleep in the dust of the earth will awake: some to everlasting life, others to shame and everlasting contempt." (Daniel 12:2)

Question 76: What is the final judgment?

The Bible teaches that history is moving toward a definitive conclusion when God will judge all humanity. This final judgment also called the day of judgment or the great white throne judgment, is when God will evaluate every person's life and render His perfect verdict.

Scripture portrays Jesus Christ as the judge. John 5:22 states, "The Father judges no one, but has entrusted all judgment to the Son." The one who died to save humanity will also be the one who judges it—a sobering and yet hopeful truth.

This judgment will be:

Universal—including every person who has ever lived (Romans 14:10-12).

Comprehensive—covering "every secret thing, whether good or evil" (Ecclesiastes 12:14) and even our words (Matthew 12:36-37).

Righteous—based on perfect knowledge and justice, without favouritism (Romans 2:5-11).

For believers, the final judgment isn't about determining salvation. Those in Christ have already passed from death to life (John 5:24). Instead, it's about evaluating our faithfulness and service, with rewards given accordingly (1 Corinthians 3:12-15; 2 Corinthians 5:10).

For unbelievers, this judgment confirms their rejection of God's grace and establishes the justice of their eternal separation from Him. Revelation 20:11-15 describes those not found in the "book of life" being consigned to the "lake of fire."

The reality of final judgment provides several vital perspectives:

- It demonstrates God's justice—sin will not ultimately go unpunished
- It establishes accountability—our choices matter eternally

- It provides comfort to the persecuted—wrongs will be made right
- It motivates evangelism—people need to be reconciled to God before judgment

While the final judgment is a solemn reality, for those in Christ it need not provoke fear. "There is now no condemnation for those who are in Christ Jesus" (Romans 8:1). The Judge is also our Savior, who bore the penalty for our sins.

Key Bible Verses:

- "For we must all appear before the judgment seat of Christ, so that each of us may receive what is due us for the things done while in the body, whether good or bad." (2 Corinthians 5:10)
- "And I saw the dead, great and small, standing before the throne, and books were opened. Another book was opened, which is the Book of Life. The dead were judged according to what they had done as recorded in the books." (Revelation 20:12)
- "This will take place on the day when God judges people's secrets through Jesus Christ, as my gospel declares." (Romans 2:16)

Question 77: What is the new heaven and new earth?

The Bible's final chapters reveal humanity's ultimate destiny isn't an ethereal heaven but a renewed physical creation—what Scripture calls "a new heaven and a new earth" (Revelation 21:1). This isn't the annihilation of the current universe but its thorough renewal and transformation.

The apostle Peter describes how "the present heavens and earth are reserved for fire, being kept for the day of judgment" (2 Peter 3:7), after which God will create "a new heaven and a new earth, where righteousness dwells" (2 Peter 3:13). This aligns with Paul's teaching that creation itself "will be liberated from its bondage to decay" (Romans 8:21).

In Revelation 21-22, John provides our fullest glimpse of this renewed creation:

God will dwell directly with His people. "God's dwelling place is now among the people, and he will dwell with them" (Revelation 21:3). The separation between heaven and earth will end as God's presence fills the renewed creation.

The New Jerusalem descends from heaven. This magnificent city represents God's people in perfect communion with Him. Its immense proportions, precious materials, and ideal symmetry symbolize the splendor of redeemed humanity's final home.

All consequences of sin are removed. "He will wipe every tear from their eyes. There will be no more death or mourning or crying or pain, for the old order of things has passed away" (Revelation 21:4). The curse that entered at the Fall will be completely reversed.

Creation is restored and perfected. The tree of life returns, "yielding its fruit every month... for the healing of the nations" (Revelation 22:2). Rivers of living water flow through the city, suggesting abundant life and fruitfulness.

This glorious future is the culmination of God's redemptive plan. Far from abandoning His physical creation, God will perfect it. This gives profound value to our current world—it's not disposable but destined for renewal. It also shapes our mission: we work for justice, beauty, and healing now as foretastes of what God will perfect in the age to come.

Key Bible Verses:

- "Then I saw 'a new heaven and a new earth,' for the first heaven and the first earth had passed away, and there was no longer any sea." (Revelation 21:1)

- "But in keeping with his promise we are looking forward to a new heaven and a new earth, where righteousness dwells." (2 Peter 3:13)

- "The creation itself will be liberated from its bondage to decay and brought into the freedom and glory of the children of God." (Romans 8:21)

Question 78: Do pets go to heaven?

Many people deeply love their pets and naturally wonder if these beloved animals will be part of the eternal future. While Scripture doesn't directly address whether specific pets are in heaven, it does provide principles that offer perspective.

First, the Bible affirms the value of animals in God's eyes. God created animals and called them "good" (Genesis 1:25). He cares for them providentially (Psalm 104:27-28) and knows when even a sparrow falls (Matthew 10:29). God instructed humans to treat animals humanely (Proverbs 12:10) and included animals in His covenant with Noah (Genesis 9:9-10).

Second, Scripture indicates animals will be part of the renewed creation. Isaiah's prophecies of the future kingdom include peaceful animals (Isaiah 11:6-9; 65:25). Romans 8:19-22 describes all creation groaning for redemption from the curse, suggesting animals participate in both the suffering of the present age and the liberation of the age to come.

Third, the new earth will likely include animals because it represents the perfection of God's original creation design, which included diverse creatures. The description in Revelation 22 echoes the Garden of Eden, where animals certainly existed.

While these principles don't specifically address whether your particular pet will be in heaven, they do suggest that animals will be part of God's renewed creation. God, who knows the number of hairs on your head, certainly understands the bond between humans and their animal companions.

Some theologians, like C.S. Lewis, have suggested that pets might be present in heaven through their relationship with humans, whose love "brings them into existence, from a sort of sub-existence." While speculative, this reflects the truth that relationships matter to God.

We can confidently say that whatever God has planned for eternity will fulfill and exceed our deepest desires for reunion, joy, and the flourishing of all creation.

Key Bible Verses:

- "The wolf will live with the lamb, the leopard will lie down with the goat, the calf and the lion and the yearling together; and a little child will lead them." (Isaiah 11:6)

- "The creation itself will be liberated from its bondage to decay and brought into the freedom and glory of the children of God." (Romans 8:21)

- "Are not five sparrows sold for two pennies? Yet not one of them is forgotten by God." (Luke 12:6)

Question 79: Will there be rewards in heaven?

Scripture clearly teaches that believers will receive different rewards in heaven based on their faithfulness in this life. This doesn't contradict salvation by grace; rather, it recognizes that while salvation is a free gift, our works matter to God and carry eternal significance.

Jesus frequently spoke of heavenly rewards. He instructed His followers to "store up for yourselves treasures in heaven" (Matthew 6:20) and promises that those who face persecution would have "great reward in heaven" (Matthew 5:12). He described varying levels of responsibility given to faithful servants (Matthew 25:14-30).

Paul elaborated on this concept, explaining that each believer's work will be tested by fire on "the Day." Works of lasting value (compared to gold, silver, and precious stones) will survive and be rewarded, while worthless works (wood, hay, straw) will be burned up. The person will be saved, but may "suffer loss" of potential reward (1 Corinthians 3:12-15).

Scripture mentions specific rewards, including:

- Crowns for various aspects of faithfulness (1 Corinthians 9:25; 1 Thessalonians 2:19; 2 Timothy 4:8)

- Positions of responsibility and authority (Luke 19:17-19)

- Special recognition from Christ (Matthew 25:21)

Several important principles apply to these rewards:

- They're based on faithfulness, not just results (Matthew 25:21)

- Even small acts of service are noticed and rewarded (Matthew 10:42)

- Pure motives matter—rewards can be lost by seeking human recognition (Matthew 6:1-6)

- Believers will ultimately cast their crowns before Christ's throne, recognizing all accomplishments as ultimately His work through them (Revelation 4:10-11)

The doctrine of rewards should inspire faithful service without promoting self-centered ambition. It reminds us that our choices now echo in eternity, and God graciously notices and values our service. As C.S. Lewis observed, "If there lurks in most modern minds the notion that to desire our own good and earnestly to hope for the enjoyment of it is a bad thing, I submit that this notion... is no part of the Christian faith."

Key Bible Verses:

- "Store up for yourselves treasures in heaven, where moths and vermin do not destroy, and where thieves do not break in and steal." (Matthew 6:20)

- "His master replied, 'Well done, good and faithful servant! You have been faithful with a few things; I will put you in charge of many things. Come and share your master's happiness!'" (Matthew 25:21)

- "If what has been built survives, the builder will receive a reward." (1 Corinthians 3:14)

Question 80: How can I be sure I'm going to heaven?

Many believers struggle with doubt about their salvation. They wonder, "Have I done enough?" or "Is my faith strong enough?" Scripture offers excellent assurance for those who trust in Christ.

First and foremost, assurance comes from understanding that salvation depends on Christ's work, not ours. We're saved "by grace... through faith—and this is not from yourselves, it is the gift of God—not by works" (Ephesians 2:8-9). Our confidence rests on Christ's perfect sacrifice, not our imperfect efforts. As Romans 8:1 declares, "There is now no condemnation for those who are in Christ Jesus."

Second, God wants you to be sure of your salvation. First John 5:13 states, "I write these things to you who believe in the name of the Son of God so that you may know that you have eternal life." This assurance isn't a presumption but the reception of God's clear promise.

Third, the Holy Spirit provides internal assurance. "The Spirit himself testifies with our spirit that we are God's children" (Romans 8:16). This isn't merely an emotional feeling but a deep conviction that you belong to God.

Fourth, genuine faith produces visible evidence. While these signs don't save us, they confirm our salvation:

- Growing love for God and others (1 John 4:7-8)

- Increasing hatred of sin and desire for holiness (Romans 7:14-25)

- Perseverance in faith despite difficulties (1 John 2:19)

- Receptivity to God's discipline (Hebrews 12:5-8)

If you've trusted Christ alone for salvation, you can have confidence in your eternal destiny. When doubts arise, return to the objective promises of Scripture rather than subjective feelings. Remember Jesus' words: "My sheep listen to my voice; I know them, and they follow me. I give them eternal life, and they shall never perish; no one will snatch them out of my hand" (John 10:27-28).

Key Bible Verses:

- "I write these things to you who believe in the name of the Son of God so that you may know that you have eternal life." (1 John 5:13)

- "For I am convinced that neither death nor life, neither angels nor demons, neither the present nor the future, nor any powers, neither height nor depth, nor anything else in all creation, will be able to separate us from the love of God that is in Christ Jesus our Lord." (Romans 8:38-39)

- "My sheep listen to my voice; I know them, and they follow me. I give them eternal life, and they shall never perish; no one will snatch them out of my hand." (John 10:27-28)

Section 9: End Times and Prophecy

Question 81: What are the "end times"?

The phrase "end times" refers to the final period of history leading to Christ's return and the establishment of God's kingdom in its fullness. Christians have varying views on these events' specific details and timelines, but Scripture provides key principles all believers can affirm.

In one sense, we've been living in the "last days" since Christ's first coming. The apostle Peter, quoting the prophet Joel, indicated that Pentecost marked the beginning of the last days (Acts 2:16-17). Hebrews 1:2 says that God "in these last days has spoken to us by his Son." This current age between Christ's first and second comings is the final chapter of history before God's kingdom comes in fullness.

However, Scripture also indicates intensifying signs and events as history climaxes. Jesus described various indicators of the approaching end, including:

- Wars and rumors of wars (Matthew 24:6)

- Natural disasters (Matthew 24:7)

- Persecution of believers (Matthew 24:9)

- Widespread deception (Matthew 24:11)

- The global proclamation of the gospel (Matthew 24:14)

Paul warned that "in the last days, difficult times will come" (2 Timothy 3:1), describing increasing godlessness, selfishness, and moral breakdown. Other passages mention the rise of a figure called the Antichrist (2 Thessalonians 2:3-4) and a period of great tribulation before Christ's return.

Christians should approach end-times teaching with balance—neither obsessing over precise timelines (which Jesus said only the Father knows—Matthew 24:36) nor ignoring prophetic Scripture. The purpose of biblical teaching about the end times isn't to satisfy curiosity but to shape our priorities and strengthen our faithfulness.

Knowing that history has a divinely appointed conclusion should inspire evangelistic urgency, holy living, and patient endurance through trials. As Peter wrote, "Since everything will be destroyed in this way, what kind of people ought you to be? You ought to live holy and godly lives as you look forward to the day of God" (2 Peter 3:11-12).

Key Bible Verses:

- "But about that day or hour no one knows, not even the angels in heaven, nor the Son, but only the Father." (Matthew 24:36)

- "This gospel of the kingdom will be preached in the whole world as a testimony to all nations, and then the end will come." (Matthew 24:14)

- "But the day of the Lord will come like a thief." (2 Peter 3:10)

Question 82: What is the rapture?

The term "rapture" describes the event when Christ returns to gather believers—both living and dead—to Himself. While the word "rapture" doesn't appear in most English Bibles, it comes from the Latin word used to translate Greek ("caught up") in 1 Thessalonians 4:17: "After that, we who are still alive and are left will be caught up together with them in the clouds to meet the Lord in the air."

This passage provides our clearest description of the rapture: Christ descends from heaven, the dead in Christ rise first, then living believers are "caught up" to meet the Lord in the air. In a related passage, Paul describes how believers will be transformed: "In a flash, in the twinkling of an eye, at the last trumpet... the dead will be raised imperishable, and we will be changed" (1 Corinthians 15:52).

While Christians agree on the reality of this event, they differ on its timing, particularly regarding its relationship to the tribulation period described in Revelation:

Pre-tribulation view: Christ will rapture the church before the tribulation begins, sparing believers from this time of judgment. This perspective sees the rapture and Christ's second coming as separate events separated by the seven-year tribulation.

Mid-tribulation view: Believers will experience the first half of the tribulation but be raptured before the most severe judgments in the second half.

Post-tribulation view: The rapture occurs at the end of the tribulation as part of Christ's visible return to establish His kingdom. In this view, believers go through the entire tribulation period.

Each position has biblical support and is held by sincere, thoughtful Christians. Rather than dividing over timing details, we can unite around the essential truth that Christ will return for His people. This "blessed hope" (Titus 2:13) encourages us to live faithfully, watching for His appearance and proclaiming His gospel until He comes.

Key Bible Verses:

- "For the Lord himself will come down from heaven, with a loud command, with the voice of the archangel and with the trumpet call of God, and the dead in Christ will rise first. After that, we who are still alive and are left will be caught up together with them in the clouds to meet the Lord in the air." (1 Thessalonians 4:16-17)

- "Listen, I tell you a mystery: We will not all sleep, but we will all be changed—in a flash, in the twinkling of an eye, at the last trumpet." (1 Corinthians 15:51-52)

- "While we wait for the blessed hope—the appearing of the glory of our great God and Savior, Jesus Christ." (Titus 2:13)

Question 83: Who is the Antichrist?

The term "Antichrist" captures the imagination and has prompted much speculation throughout church history. Scripture offers essential insights into this figure, though many details remain mysterious.

The word "antichrist" appears only in John's letters (1 John 2:18, 22; 4:3; 2 John 1:7), referring to a specific future figure and a spirit of opposition to Christ evident in false teachers. John writes, "You have heard that the antichrist is coming, even now many antichrists have come" (1 John 2:18).

Other passages describe a powerful end-times figure who opposes God, though using different terms:

- The "man of lawlessness" who "opposes and exalts himself over everything that is called God" (2 Thessalonians 2:3-4)
- The "beast" from Revelation 13, who receives power from the dragon (Satan) and is worshiped by the world
- Daniel's prophecies mention a "little horn" with similar characteristics (Daniel 7:8, 24-25)

Combining these passages, we can identify several features of the Antichrist:

- He will oppose God and exalt himself, even claiming to be divine
- He will deceive many through false signs and wonders
- He will persecute God's people
- He will have great but temporary political power
- He will ultimately be defeated by Christ at His return

Throughout history, many individuals have been identified as the Antichrist—various Roman emperors, popes, political leaders, and cultural figures. However, such definitive identifications have consistently proven premature and misguided.

While being aware of this biblical teaching, Christians should avoid obsession with identifying the Antichrist. Jesus emphasized readiness for His return rather than decoding every prophetic detail. The most important response to this teaching is faithfulness to Christ regardless of opposition or deception. As John wrote, the way to overcome antichrists is to "remain in what you have heard from the beginning" (1 John 2:24)—the true gospel of Jesus Christ.

Key Bible Verses:

- "Dear children, this is the last hour; and as you have heard that the antichrist is coming, even now many antichrists have come." (1 John 2:18)

- "Don't let anyone deceive you in any way, for that day will not come until the rebellion occurs and the man of lawlessness is revealed, the man doomed to destruction." (2 Thessalonians 2:3)
- "The beast was given a mouth to utter proud words and blasphemies and to exercise its authority for forty-two months." (Revelation 13:5)

Question 84: What is the tribulation?

The tribulation refers to a future period of unprecedented trouble and suffering that will precede Christ's return. Jesus described it as "great distress, unequaled from the beginning of the world until now—and never to be equaled again" (Matthew 24:21).

The most detailed information about this period comes from the book of Revelation, where chapters 6-19 describe a series of judgments (seals, trumpets, and bowls) poured out on a rebellious world. Many scholars connect this period with Daniel's prophecy of a final "seven-year period" (Daniel 9:27), during which a powerful leader will make and then break a covenant with Israel.

This tribulation period will feature:

- Intensified natural disasters and ecological crises
- Widespread war and violence
- Economic instability and oppressive political control
- Severe persecution of believers
- False religious systems that oppose true faith
- God's judgments on unrepentant humanity

Scripture suggests several purposes for this difficult time:

- To reveal the true nature of human rebellion against God
- To offer a final opportunity for repentance before judgment
- To refine and purify believers through testing
- To demonstrate God's righteous judgment of sin
- To set the stage for Christ's triumphant return

Christians hold different views about whether the church will experience this tribulation:

- Pre-tribulationists believe believers will be raptured before it begins
- Mid-tribulationists expect the rapture halfway through the seven years
- Post-tribulationists believe Christians will endure the entire period, being divinely sustained through it

Whatever position we take, Scripture clearly teaches that God protects His people spiritually even when they experience physical suffering. Revelation shows that many will come to faith during this period despite (or because of) its intensity, and it culminates in Christ's victorious return to establish His kingdom.

Key Bible Verses:

- "For then there will be great distress, unequaled from the beginning of the world until now—and never to be equaled again." (Matthew 24:21)

- "He will confirm a covenant with many for one 'seven.' In the middle of the 'seven' he will put an end to sacrifice and offering." (Daniel 9:27)

- "If those days had not been cut short, no one would survive, but for the sake of the elect those days will be shortened." (Matthew 24:22)

Question 85: What are the signs of Christ's return?

One of the disciples' last questions to Jesus was about the sign of His coming (Matthew 24:3). In response, Jesus provided important indicators while emphasizing that no one knows the exact day or hour (Matthew 24:36).

Scripture reveals several signs that will precede Christ's return:

Widespread deception. Jesus warned that "many false prophets will appear and deceive many people" (Matthew 24:11). As His return approaches, spiritual deception will increase, with false messiahs and misleading teachings.

Global turmoil. Jesus spoke of "wars and rumors of wars," along with "famines and earthquakes in various places" (Matthew 24:6-7). While such calamities occur throughout history, their intensity and frequency will escalate.

Moral decline. Paul predicted that "in the last days... people will be lovers of themselves, lovers of money, boastful, proud" and marked by various forms of godlessness (2 Timothy 3:1-5). Society will increasingly reject God's moral standards.

Persecution of believers. Jesus says, "You will be handed over to be persecuted and put to death, and you will be hated by all nations because of me" (Matthew 24:9). The Christian faith will face growing hostility worldwide.

Global evangelism. Despite opposition, "this gospel of the kingdom will be preached in the whole world as a testimony to all nations, and then the end will come" (Matthew 24:14). The Great Commission must be fulfilled before Christ returns.

Israel's restoration. Many scholars see prophetic significance in Israel's modern rebirth and Jerusalem's restoration to Jewish control, based on passages like Luke 21:24.

While watching for these signs, we should maintain balance. Jesus warned against both ignorance ("like a thief in the night" for the unprepared—1 Thessalonians 5:2-4) and obsessive date-setting (Matthew 24:36). Our primary response should be faithful readiness: "So you also must be ready, because the Son of Man will come at an hour when you do not expect him" (Matthew 24:44).

Key Bible Verses:

- "What will be the sign of your coming and of the end of the age?" (Matthew 24:3)
- "No one knows about that day or hour, not even the angels in heaven, nor the Son, but only the Father." (Matthew 24:36)
- "So you also must be ready, because the Son of Man will come at an hour when you do not expect him." (Matthew 24:44)

Question 86: What is the millennium?

The millennium refers to the thousand-year reign of Christ described in Revelation 20:1-6: "They came to life and reigned with Christ a thousand years." During this period, Satan is bound, and believers rule with Christ in unprecedented peace and righteousness.

Christians hold three major views about the millennium based on different interpretations of Revelation and related passages:

Premillennialism teaches that Christ will return physically to earth before (pre-) the millennium begins. He will establish a literal thousand-year kingdom, fulfilling promises to Israel and ruling with resurrected saints. After this period, there will be a final rebellion, judgment, and the eternal state. This was the dominant view of the early church.

Postmillennialism holds that Christ will return after (post-) the millennium. According to this view, the millennium represents a golden age of Christian influence when the gospel progressively transforms society. Once the world has mainly been Christianized, Christ will return to establish the eternal state.

Amillennialism (literally "no millennium") interprets the thousand years symbolically, representing the entire church age between Christ's first and second comings. Satan is currently restricted (bound) in his ability to deceive the nations, while deceased believers reign with Christ in heaven. This period ends with Christ's return for final judgment.

Each view has strengths and weaknesses, and sincere Christians can differ in their understanding. What's most important is what all these positions affirm:

- Christ will personally, visibly return to earth
- Evil will ultimately be defeated and judged
- God's kingdom will be established in its fullness
- Believers will share in Christ's victory and reign

The millennium reminds us that history has a purpose and direction. God is working to establish His kingdom—partially now through the church, but completely when Christ returns. This hope gives meaning to our present struggles and inspires faithful service as we anticipate the fulfillment of God's promises.

Key Bible Verses:

- "Blessed and holy are those who share in the first resurrection. The second death has no power over them, but they will be priests of God and of Christ and will reign with him for a thousand years." (Revelation 20:6)

- "Your kingdom come, your will be done, on earth as it is in heaven." (Matthew 6:10)

- "The kingdom of the world has become the kingdom of our Lord and of his Messiah, and he will reign for ever and ever." (Revelation 11:15)

Question 87: What is the Book of Revelation about?

The Book of Revelation, the final book of the Bible, can seem intimidating with its vivid symbolism and apocalyptic imagery. However, understanding its basic purpose and structure makes it more accessible and spiritually valuable.

Revelation was written by the apostle John while exiled on the island of Patmos, probably around AD 95 during the persecution under Emperor Domitian. The book identifies itself as "the revelation [unveiling] of Jesus Christ" (Revelation 1:1), showing it primarily reveals Jesus in His glory and final victory.

The book has several key purposes:

- To comfort persecuted believers with the assurance of Christ's ultimate triumph

- To warn complacent Christians about the dangers of compromise with the surrounding culture

- To reveal God's perspective on human history and its culmination

- To invite worship and renewed commitment to Christ

Revelation's structure includes:

- Letters to seven historical churches, containing both commendation and criticism (chapters 1-3)

- Visions of heavenly worship, emphasizing God's sovereignty (chapters 4-5)

- Three cycles of judgments—seals, trumpets, and bowls—showing God's response to human rebellion (chapters 6-16)

- The fall of "Babylon" (representing anti-God systems) and the defeat of the beast and false prophet (chapters 17-19)

- The millennium, final judgment, and new heaven and earth (chapters 20-22)

Interpreting Revelation requires recognizing its genre as apocalyptic literature, which uses symbolic language to convey spiritual truths. Some symbols are explained in the text itself (Revelation 1:20), while others draw on Old Testament imagery that would have been familiar to early readers.

Christians approach Revelation through different interpretive frameworks:

- Preterists believe it primarily describes events in the first-century Roman Empire
- Historicists see it as outlining the entire church age from the first century to Christ's return
- Futurists interpret most of the book as describing end-time events still to come
- Idealists view it as symbolically depicting the ongoing conflict between good and evil throughout history

Despite these differences, all Christians can agree on Revelation's central message: despite present difficulties, Jesus Christ will return in victory, evil will be defeated, and God's people will enjoy His presence forever.

Key Bible Verses:

- "The revelation from Jesus Christ, which God gave him to show his servants what must soon take place." (Revelation 1:1)
- "To the one who is victorious, I will give the right to sit with me on my throne, just as I was victorious and sat down with my Father on his throne." (Revelation 3:21)
- "Look, I am coming soon! My reward is with me, and I will give to each person according to what they have done." (Revelation 22:12)

Question 88: Will everyone have a chance to hear the Gospel before Jesus returns?

This vital question touches on both God's justice and our missionary responsibility. Jesus linked His return to global evangelism when He says, "This gospel of the kingdom will be preached in the whole world as a testimony to all nations, and then the end will come" (Matthew 24:14).

The Greek word for "nations" refers to people groups or ethnic groups rather than political nations. This suggests the gospel must reach every distinct cultural and linguistic group before Christ returns, not necessarily every individual person.

Several biblical principles help us understand this issue:

God is perfectly just. His judgment will be fair and appropriate, considering the light people have received (Romans 2:12-16). Those with greater knowledge bear greater responsibility.

God desires everyone's salvation. Scripture clearly states that God "wants all people to be saved and to come to a knowledge of the truth" (1 Timothy 2:4). He is "not wanting anyone to perish, but everyone to come to repentance" (2 Peter 3:9).

God's timing considers evangelism. Peter suggests the Lord's apparent "slowness" in returning is related to His desire that more would repent (2 Peter 3:9). He is giving time for the gospel to spread.

We have a crucial role in this process. Christ commissioned His followers to "go and make disciples of all nations" (Matthew 28:19). Our obedience, or lack thereof, affects how quickly all people hear the good news.

While we can't definitively say every individual will hear the gospel before death, we can affirm that God's judgment will be perfectly fair. Those who never had the opportunity to hear about Christ will be judged according to the light they did receive and how they responded to God's revelation in creation and conscience (Romans 1:19-20; 2:14-15).

Rather than speculating, our response should be urgent in fulfilling the Great Commission. Nearly 2,000 years after Christ's command, thousands of people groups still lack a clear gospel witness. We can participate in God's plan to reach all nations through prayer, giving, going, and sending.

Key Bible Verses:

- "This gospel of the kingdom will be preached in the whole world as a testimony to all nations, and then the end will come." (Matthew 24:14)

- "The Lord is not slow in keeping his promise, as some understand slowness. Instead he is patient with you, not wanting anyone to perish, but everyone to come to repentance." (2 Peter 3:9)

- "How, then, can they call on the one they have not believed in? And how can they believe in the one of whom they have not heard? And how can they hear without someone preaching to them?" (Romans 10:14)

Question 89: How should Christians live in light of the end times?

The Bible's teachings about the end times aren't meant merely to satisfy curiosity about the future but to transform how we live in the present. Scripture provides clear guidance for believers awaiting Christ's return.

First, maintain watchful readiness. Jesus emphasized this repeatedly: "Therefore keep watch, because you do not know on what day your Lord will come" (Matthew 24:42). This doesn't mean obsessing over signs or setting dates but living with awareness that Christ could return at any moment.

Second, pursue holiness and godly character. Peter asks, "Since everything will be destroyed in this way, what kind of people ought you to be? You ought to live holy and godly lives as you look forward to the day of God" (2 Peter 3:11-12). Knowing that Christ will evaluate our lives should motivate pure living.

Third, be faithful in your God-given responsibilities. In Jesus' parable, the master commends servants who continue working diligently during his absence (Matthew 24:45-47). This includes both personal ministry and everyday tasks—family, work, and community obligations.

Fourth, prioritize evangelism and missions. Jesus' return awaits the completion of global gospel proclamation (Matthew 24:14). We should urgently share Christ with others while there's still time.

Fifth, maintain perspective during suffering. End-times teaching reminds us that present hardships are temporary. Paul wrote, "I consider that our present sufferings are not worth comparing with the glory that will be revealed in us" (Romans 8:18).

Sixth, encourage one another with these truths. Paul instructed believers to "encourage each other with these words" about Christ's return (1 Thessalonians 4:18). End-times teaching should build up the church, not create division.

Seventh, stay balanced. Avoid both extremes of ignoring prophecy and becoming obsessed with it. Focus on the clear essentials while holding secondary details with humility.

These principles apply regardless of which specific end-times viewpoint you hold. The most important question isn't exactly when or how Christ will return, but whether you'll be found faithful when He does.

Key Bible Verses:

- "So you also must be ready, because the Son of Man will come at an hour when you do not expect him." (Matthew 24:44)

- "Since everything will be destroyed in this way, what kind of people ought you to be? You ought to live holy and godly lives." (2 Peter 3:11)

- "Encourage each other with these words." (1 Thessalonians 4:18)

Question 90: What is the ultimate hope of Christians regarding the future?

While Christians may differ on details of end-times prophecy, we share a common, glorious hope that Scripture presents with striking clarity.

Our ultimate hope centers on Jesus Christ Himself. Paul calls this "the blessed hope—the appearing of the glory of our great God and Savior, Jesus Christ" (Titus 2:13). Our deepest longing isn't just for heaven or blessings but for Christ Himself—to see Him face to face and be with Him forever.

This hope includes several magnificent promises:

The visible, personal return of Christ. Jesus promises, "I will come back and take you to be with me" (John 14:3). He will return not as a spiritual influence but bodily, visibly, and gloriously.

Resurrection and transformation. Believers who have died will be raised, and those still alive will be transformed—all receiving glorified bodies like Christ's (Philippians 3:20-21). These resurrection bodies will be physical yet perfect, immune to sickness, aging, and death.

Perfect communion with God. Revelation describes how "God's dwelling place is now among the people, and he will dwell with them" (Revelation 21:3). The barrier of sin that limited our relationship with God will be completely removed.

The renewal of all creation. God will establish "a new heaven and a new earth" (Revelation 21:1), freeing creation from corruption and decay (Romans 8:21). This isn't the destruction of the physical world but its purification and perfection.

Justice and peace. God will make all things right, wiping away every tear and ending all suffering (Revelation 21:4). Christ will rule with perfect justice and wisdom.

This hope distinguishes Christianity from both secular pessimism (which sees only environmental catastrophe or cosmic meaninglessness ahead) and shallow optimism (which believes human progress will solve all problems). The Christian hope depends not on human achievement but on God's faithfulness to His promises.

This future hope gives meaning, direction, and courage for the present. As C.S. Lewis observed, "If you read history you will find that the Christians who did most for the present world were precisely those who thought most of the next."

Key Bible Verses:

- "While we wait for the blessed hope—the appearing of the glory of our great God and Savior, Jesus Christ." (Titus 2:13)

- "When Christ, who is your life, appears, then you also will appear with him in glory." (Colossians 3:4)

- "He who testifies to these things says, 'Yes, I am coming soon.' Amen. Come, Lord Jesus." (Revelation 22:20)

Section 10: Faith in the Real World

Question 91: Why does God allow suffering and evil?

This question touches on the deepest human pain and confusion. While Scripture doesn't provide a simple answer, it offers several insights to help us navigate this rugged terrain.

First, suffering entered our world through human sin. Genesis 3 shows how humanity's rebellion against God fractured our relationship with Him, with each other, and with creation itself. We live in a fallen world where disease, natural disasters, and human cruelty are realities—not part of God's original design.

Second, God allows human freedom, which makes genuine love possible and permits real evil. Much suffering comes from people misusing their freedom to harm others.

Third, God can work through suffering to accomplish greater purposes:

- To develop our character and faith (Romans 5:3-4; James 1:2-4)

- To draw us closer to Him (Psalm 119:71)

- To equip us to comfort others (2 Corinthians 1:3-4)

- To display His power through our weakness (2 Corinthians 12:9)

Most importantly, God understands suffering firsthand. In Jesus, God entered our broken world and experienced betrayal, rejection, torture, and death. Hebrews 4:15-16 assures us that Jesus can "empathize with our weaknesses" and invites us to "approach God's throne of grace with confidence."

Finally, God promises to end all suffering. Revelation 21:4 describes a future where He "will wipe every tear from their eyes. There will be no more death or mourning or crying or pain."

Until that day, we can trust that God remains present in our pain, working even through difficult circumstances to fulfill His good purposes.

Key Bible Verses:

- "And we know that in all things God works for the good of those who love him, who have been called according to his purpose." (Romans 8:28)

- "For our light and momentary troubles are achieving for us an eternal glory that far outweighs them all." (2 Corinthians 4:17)

- "He will wipe every tear from their eyes. There will be no more death or mourning or crying or pain, for the old order of things has passed away." (Revelation 21:4)

Question 92: Is Christianity the only true religion?

In our pluralistic society, the Christian claim that Jesus is "the way and the truth and the life" and that "no one comes to the Father except through me" (John 14:6) can seem narrow or exclusive. Yet this teaching lies at the heart of the Christian message.

When examining this question, several vital distinctions help frame the discussion:

Christianity acknowledges partial truth in other religions. Many faiths contain moral and philosophical insights that align with reality. Paul recognized that even pagan poets occasionally expressed truth (Acts 17:28). However, containing elements of truth doesn't make a belief system entirely true.

Christianity makes unique claims about Jesus Christ. While other religions may honour Jesus as a prophet or teacher, Christianity alone recognizes Him as the divine Son of God who died for humanity's sins and rose from the dead. These aren't minor theological details but the very foundation of Christian faith.

Christianity addresses our fundamental problem differently. Most religions present some version of human effort—moral improvement, spiritual disciplines, religious rituals—as the path to salvation. Christianity uniquely teaches that we cannot save ourselves; only God's grace through Christ's sacrifice can rescue us.

Christianity is based on historical events, not just philosophical concepts. The truth of Christianity hinges on the actual resurrection of Jesus (1 Corinthians 15:14-19). If Christ rose from the dead as the Gospels claim, this validates His teachings, including His exclusive claims.

This exclusive truth claim doesn't mean Christians should be arrogant or disrespectful toward other faiths. Jesus calls His followers to love all people, including those with different beliefs. Christians can simultaneously hold firm convictions about truth while showing genuine respect and compassion for everyone.

The exclusivity of Christ highlights the inclusivity of the gospel invitation. Jesus offers salvation to people "from every nation, tribe, people and language" (Revelation 7:9) regardless of their background, social status, or past actions. Anyone who comes to Him in faith will be welcomed.

Key Bible Verses:

- "Jesus answered, 'I am the way and the truth and the life. No one comes to the Father except through me.'" (John 14:6)

- "Salvation is found in no one else, for there is no other name under heaven given to mankind by which we must be saved." (Acts 4:12)

- "For there is one God and one mediator between God and mankind, the man Christ Jesus." (1 Timothy 2:5)

Question 93: Hasn't science disproved the Bible?

Popular media often portrays science and the Bible as fundamentally at odds, suggesting that modern discoveries have rendered Scripture obsolete or false. However, this perceived conflict largely rests on misunderstandings of both science and the Bible.

First, it's essential to recognize that science and the Bible address different primary questions. Science focuses on how the natural world works through observable, testable processes. The Bible addresses who created the world, why we exist, and how we should live. These are complementary rather than competing with realms of knowledge.

Second, the Bible wasn't written as a scientific textbook. It uses phenomenological language (describing things as they appear to human observers) rather than technical terminology. For example, phrases like "the sun rising" reflect how we experience the world, just as modern meteorologists might talk about "sunrise" without denying that the Earth rotates around the sun.

Third, many supposed conflicts arise from interpretive mistakes on both sides:

- Misinterpreting biblical passages by imposing modern scientific questions on ancient texts

- Overextending scientific theories beyond what the evidence demonstrates

- Confusing methodological naturalism (science's practical focus on natural causes) with philosophical naturalism (the claim that nothing exists beyond the natural world)

Fourth, many pioneering scientists throughout history were devout believers who saw no conflict between their faith and scientific inquiry. Figures like Galileo, Newton, Faraday, Pasteur, and modern scientists like Francis Collins have integrated their Christian faith with rigorous scientific work.

While specific tensions exist between certain interpretations of Scripture and certain scientific theories, these often create healthy dialogue rather than irresolvable conflict. For example, Christians hold various perspectives on questions like the age of the earth or the mechanisms of creation while maintaining core biblical beliefs about God as Creator.

Far from disproving the Bible, many scientific discoveries align with biblical descriptions: the universe having a beginning, the fine-tuning of physical constants, the complexity of biological information, and the unique capacities of human consciousness all point to an intelligent Creator rather than mere chance.

Key Bible Verses:

- "The heavens declare the glory of God; the skies proclaim the work of his hands." (Psalm 19:1)

- "For since the creation of the world God's invisible qualities—his eternal power and divine nature—have been clearly seen, being understood from what has been made." (Romans 1:20)

- "By faith we understand that the universe was formed at God's command, so that what is seen was not made out of what was visible." (Hebrews 11:3)

Question 94: Is the Bible full of contradictions?

Critics often claim the Bible contains irreconcilable contradictions that undermine its reliability and divine inspiration. While Scripture does contain challenging passages that require careful study, alleged contradictions typically dissolve when examined with proper interpretive principles.

Several key considerations help resolve apparent discrepancies:

Different perspectives don't equal contradictions. The Gospels sometimes record the same event with varying details—just as multiple witnesses to an accident might emphasize different aspects while describing the same reality. For example, the accounts of how many angels were at Jesus' tomb (one or two) simply reflect different levels of detail, not contradiction.

Ancient writing used different standards than modern technical precision. Numbers might be rounded, quotations weren't expected to be verbatim, and events weren't always narrated in strict chronological order. Judging ancient texts by modern journalistic standards creates artificial problems.

Context matters tremendously. Many alleged contradictions arise from ignoring historical, literary, or situational context. For instance, Paul's statements about faith and work seem contradictory only when removed from their specific contexts, which address different questions.

Translation issues can create apparent problems. What seems contradictory in English may not be in the original Hebrew or Greek. Different words might be translated the same way in English, obscuring important distinctions in the original languages.

Some passages use different literary genres. Poetry, apocalyptic visions, and historical narratives each follow different conventions. When Psalm 50 says God owns "the cattle on a thousand hills," it's poetic language about God's ownership of everything, not a literal inventory of divine livestock.

Careful study has resolved countless alleged contradictions throughout church history. Resources like Bible commentaries and study Bibles can help readers navigate challenging passages. More importantly, the theological and moral cohesion of Scripture across various authors, cultures, and centuries testifies to its divine inspiration despite human authorship.

Rather than being discouraged by difficult passages, we can approach them with patience, humility, and confidence that reasonable explanations exist, even if we don't immediately see them.

Key Bible Verses:

- "All Scripture is God-breathed and is useful for teaching, rebuking, correcting and training in righteousness." (2 Timothy 3:16)
- "Your word is truth." (John 17:17)
- "The word of God is alive and active." (Hebrews 4:12)

Question 95: Isn't the Bible outdated or culturally irrelevant?

Some dismiss the Bible as a relic of ancient times, irrelevant to modern life and ethical questions. Yet billions of people across diverse cultures still find Scripture remarkably applicable to contemporary challenges. How can a collection of writings from thousands of years ago remain relevant today?

First, the Bible addresses timeless human needs and questions. While technology and cultural expressions change, fundamental aspects of human nature remain consistent. People still seek meaning, struggle with relationships, face moral dilemmas, experience suffering, and wonder about life after death. Scripture speaks directly to these enduring realities.

Second, biblical principles transcend their cultural settings. While the Bible contains culturally specific elements (like ancient Near Eastern legal codes), it also teaches overarching principles that cross cultural boundaries. For example, "love your neighbor as yourself" (Leviticus 19:18) remains ethically relevant regardless of time or place.

Third, Scripture provides moral wisdom for new ethical challenges. The Bible may not explicitly address genetic engineering or artificial intelligence, but it offers principles about human dignity, stewardship of creation, and the limits of human authority that guide ethical reasoning in these areas.

Fourth, the Bible demonstrates remarkable psychological insight. Long before modern psychology, Scripture accurately described human motivation, self-deception, patterns of temptation, and pathways to emotional healing. Many therapists recognize the psychological wisdom embedded in biblical narratives and teachings.

Fifth, the Bible's transformative impact continues worldwide. Scripture still catalyzes personal and social change—from addiction recovery to reconciliation efforts in war-torn regions. This ongoing influence suggests its message connects deeply with human needs across cultural divides.

Rather than dismissing Scripture's relevance, perhaps today's readers should approach it with both respectful awareness of its ancient context and openness to its potential wisdom for contemporary challenges. As the writer of Hebrews observed, "The word of God is alive and active" (Hebrews 4:12)—not a static artifact but a living message.

Key Bible Verses:

- "The grass withers and the flowers fall, but the word of our God endures forever." (Isaiah 40:8)

- "All Scripture is God-breathed and is useful for teaching, rebuking, correcting and training in righteousness." (2 Timothy 3:16)

- "Heaven and earth will pass away, but my words will never pass away." (Matthew 24:35)

Question 96: What about people who never hear the Gospel?

This question touches deep concerns about God's justice and the fate of those who never have opportunity to hear about Jesus Christ. It's a question that should be approached with both theological faithfulness and compassionate sensitivity.

Scripture clearly teaches that salvation comes through Christ alone. Jesus says, "I am the way and the truth and the life. No one comes to the father except through me" (John 14:6). Acts 4:12 affirms there is "no other name under heaven given to mankind by which we must be saved."

At the same time, the Bible reveals that God is perfectly just (Deuteronomy 32:4) and "does not show favoritism" (Acts 10:34). He judges people based on the light they have received. Romans 2:12-16 suggest that those without access to special revelation are judged according to their response to general revelation and conscience.

Several principles help us think about this challenging question:

God desires all people to be saved. Scripture repeatedly emphasizes God's universal love and desire that "all people be saved and come to a knowledge of the truth" (1 Timothy 2:4). He is "not wanting anyone to perish" (2 Peter 3:9).

God's judgment is always based on perfect knowledge and justice. Unlike human judges with limited information, God understands every circumstance, opportunity, and heart attitude (1 Samuel 16:7).

God has provided general revelation to all people. Romans 1:19-20 explains that God's "invisible qualities... have been clearly seen, being understood from what has been made." While this revelation is sufficient to make people accountable, it may not provide all that's needed for salvation.

The Bible records instances of God reaching people through dreams, visions, and other extraordinary means. From Cornelius in Acts 10 to testimonies from closed countries today, God sometimes works beyond ordinary evangelistic methods to reach sincere seekers.

While we can't definitively answer all aspects of this question, we can trust in God's perfect justice and mercy. Rather than using this issue to avoid evangelism, we should be motivated to greater missionary effort, ensuring as many as possible hear the good news clearly.

Key Bible Verses:

- "God does not show favoritism but accepts from every nation the one who fears him and does what is right." (Acts 10:34-35)

- "From one man he made all the nations... God did this so that they would seek him and perhaps reach out for him and find him, though he is not far from any one of us." (Acts 17:26-27)

- "How, then, can they call on the one they have not believed in? And how can they believe in the one of whom they have not heard?" (Romans 10:14)

Question 97: Can a Christian lose their salvation?

Few questions generate more discussion among sincere believers than whether salvation, once received, can be lost. Christians throughout history have held different views on this important topic, all seeking to be faithful to Scripture's teaching.

Those who believe genuine salvation cannot be lost point to passages like:

- John 10:28-29, where Jesus says no one can snatch His sheep from His hand

- Romans 8:38-39, which states nothing can separate us from God's love in Christ

- Philippians 1:6, affirming that God will complete the good work He began in us

- Ephesians 1:13-14, describing the Holy Spirit as a "seal" and "deposit" guaranteeing our inheritance

Those who believe salvation can be lost or abandoned reference:

- Hebrews 6:4-6, warning about those who "fall away" after experiencing spiritual blessings

- 2 Peter 2:20-22, describing those who escape the world's corruption through Christ but then return to it

- Revelation 3:5, mentioning the possibility of names being blotted out of the book of life

- Jesus' warnings about being cut off from the vine (John 15:1-6)

How might we think carefully about this issue? Several considerations help:

First, distinguishing between a genuine, saving relationship with Christ and a mere religious profession is crucial. First, John 2:19 indicates that some who leave the faith "were not really of us" to begin with.

Second, eternal security should never promote complacency or license to sin. Scripture consistently calls believers to "work out your salvation with fear and trembling" (Philippians 2:12) and to "make your calling and election sure" (2 Peter 1:10).

Third, genuine faith perseveres. Those truly born of God continue in faith, even through struggles and doubts. Perseverance isn't what earns salvation but what demonstrates its reality.

While Christians may disagree on this doctrine, we can agree that salvation is entirely by God's grace through faith in Christ, that genuine believers should show evidence of spiritual transformation, and that no one should presume on God's grace by deliberately continuing in sin.

Key Bible Verses:

- "I give them eternal life, and they shall never perish; no one will snatch them out of my hand." (John 10:28)

- "They went out from us, but they did not really belong to us. For if they had belonged to us, they would have remained with us." (1 John 2:19)

- "Therefore, my brothers and sisters, make every effort to confirm your calling and election." (2 Peter 1:10)

Question 98: Are Christians hypocrites?

The charge of hypocrisy is one of the most common criticisms levelled against Christians and the church. Given the moral failures of prominent believers and the gap between Christian ideals and actual behaviour, is this criticism fair?

First, it's essential to understand what hypocrisy is. Hypocrisy isn't merely failing to live up to one's standards—it's pretending to be virtuous while deliberately concealing or excusing one's sins. Jesus reserved His harshest criticism for religious leaders who created an outward appearance of righteousness while inwardly remaining corrupt (Matthew 23:27-28).

Christianity itself acknowledges human moral weakness. The gospel begins with the recognition that "all have sinned and fall short of the glory of God" (Romans 3:23). Christians aren't people who claim moral perfection but those who recognize their need for grace and forgiveness. As the saying goes, the church is not a showcase for saints but a hospital for sinners.

Christians should be characterized by growing consistency between belief and behaviour. James warns against being merely hearers of the Word without being doers (James 1:22). Paul urges believers to "live a life worthy of the calling you have received" (Ephesians 4:1). Authentic faith should produce increasing integrity.

When Christians fall into hypocrisy, the appropriate response is repentance and a renewed commitment to integrity. This means:

- Honestly acknowledging failures rather than covering them up

- Taking responsibility rather than blaming others

- Seeking forgiveness and making amends where possible

- Remaining open to accountability and correction

Non-Christians sometimes use Christian moral failures as an excuse to reject the faith. Yet logically, the failure of Christians to live up to their ideals doesn't invalidate Christianity's truth claims—it simply confirms the Christian teaching about human sinfulness and the need for grace.

The most compelling answer to the charge of hypocrisy isn't defensive arguments but authentic, humble discipleship that demonstrates genuine transformation while honestly acknowledging ongoing struggles.

Key Bible Verses:

- "Woe to you, teachers of the law and Pharisees, you hypocrites! You are like whitewashed tombs, which look beautiful on the outside but on the inside are full of the bones of the dead and everything unclean." (Matthew 23:27)
- "Do not merely listen to the word, and so deceive yourselves. Do what it says." (James 1:22)
- "If we claim to be without sin, we deceive ourselves and the truth is not in us." (1 John 1:8)

Question 99: Isn't Christianity just a crutch?

Some critics dismiss Christianity as a psychological crutch—a comforting illusion for those unable to face life's harsh realities without supernatural support. Is faith merely wishful thinking for the weak-minded?

This criticism misses several important points:

First, if God exists, then relying on Him isn't a crutch but wisdom. C.S. Lewis noted that dismissing Christianity as wishful thinking assumes it's false: "If Christianity is comfort, it is not on that account false... If it's true, it's of supreme importance. And if it's false, it's of no importance."

Second, Christianity often makes life more challenging, not less. Following Jesus may involve sacrifice, persecution, countercultural values, and moral demands that would be easier to avoid. Many Christian converts have discovered that faith brought greater challenges rather than easy comfort.

Third, everyone relies on something for meaning and support. Secular philosophies also function as "crutches" in providing frameworks for understanding life. The question isn't whether we lean on something but whether what we lean on is accurate and reliable.

Fourth, Christianity attracted many intellectually rigorous believers throughout history. From Augustine to Aquinas to modern thinkers like Alvin Plantinga, many brilliant minds found Christianity intellectually satisfying, not emotionally comforting.

Fifth, Christianity addresses reality in all its dimensions—including the harsh realities of suffering and evil and the persistent human longing for meaning and transcendence. Rather than providing cheap comfort, it offers a profound explanation for why the world is beautiful and broken.

Perhaps what critics call a "crutch" is better understood as medicine. We don't criticize ill people for taking necessary medication; we recognize their wisdom in addressing their condition. Christianity claims all humans suffer from spiritual brokenness, and faith in Christ is the remedy—not a psychological illusion but the appropriate response to our actual condition.

Key Bible Verses:

- "For the message of the cross is foolishness to those who are perishing, but to us who are being saved it is the power of God." (1 Corinthians 1:18)

- "Come to me, all you who are weary and burdened, and I will give you rest." (Matthew 11:28)

- "Then you will know the truth, and the truth will set you free." (John 8:32)

Question 100: Can I question my faith and still be a Christian?

Faith often coexists with questions and doubts. Many Christians worry that their uncertainties indicate spiritual failure or even loss of salvation. Yet the Bible reveals that questions and struggles are standard parts of an authentic faith journey.

Scripture contains numerous examples of faithful people who questioned God:

- Abraham questioned God's justice regarding Sodom (Genesis 18:25)

- Job persistently questioned God's ways throughout his suffering

- David frequently asked "why" and "how long" in the Psalms

- Thomas doubted reports of Jesus' resurrection until he saw evidence (John 20:24-29)

- Even John the Baptist, whom Jesus called the greatest born among women, sent questions from prison about whether Jesus was truly the Messiah (Matthew 11:2-3)

Jesus didn't rebuke honest questioners but responded with patience and evidence. He gently corrected Thomas while providing the proof he needed. He answered John the Baptist by pointing to the evidence of His ministry. The father cries, "I do believe; help me overcome my unbelief!" (Mark 9:24) received Jesus' compassion and help, not condemnation.

Important distinctions exist between different types of doubt:

- Intellectual questions seeking understanding can strengthen faith when pursued with humility

- Emotional doubts during suffering may reflect honest struggle rather than unbelief

- Moral questioning that justifies sin is more concerning than sincere wrestling with difficult issues

Questioning often serves as a pathway to deeper faith. Doubt becomes dangerous only when it becomes a permanent position rather than a journey toward truth. As the philosopher Alister McGrath observed, "Doubt is not the opposite of faith; it is one element of faith."

If you're experiencing doubt, consider these approaches:

- Express your questions honestly to God in prayer
- Study Scripture, particularly passages addressing your concerns
- Seek wisdom from mature believers and thoughtful resources
- Remember that feelings of doubt don't negate the reality of your relationship with God
- Continue practicing spiritual disciplines even during seasons of uncertainty

Key Bible Verses:

- "If any of you lacks wisdom, you should ask God, who gives generously to all without finding fault, and it will be given to you." (James 1:5)
- "I do believe; help me overcome my unbelief!" (Mark 9:24)
- "Be merciful to those who doubt." (Jude 22)

Conclusion

Throughout the pages of this book, we've walked together through some of the most important, complex, and heartfelt questions people ask about God, the Bible, and the Christian life. Whether these questions arose from curiosity, crisis, or a deep hunger for spiritual truth, each one points to something essential: we are created to know, love, and walk with the living God.

The Christian faith does not demand blind belief or discourage hard questions. Instead, it welcomes sincere seekers. God invites us to bring our doubts, hopes, pain, and wonder into conversation with Him through His Word. As Jesus once says, "Ask and it will be given to you; seek and you will find; knock and the door will be opened to you" (Matthew 7:7, NIV).

As you've seen, the Bible doesn't shy away from life's toughest topics. It speaks clearly and compassion about suffering, sin, salvation, sexuality, eternity, and our everyday struggles. More than that, it speaks with authority—because it is not merely a human book but the inspired Word of God. God has spoken timeless truth into a broken world through the voices of prophets, kings, fishermen, and apostles.

This book is not the end of the journey but a signpost pointing to something greater: a living relationship with Jesus Christ. He is not just the answer to our questions—He is the ultimate answer, the Word made flesh (John 1:14), who came to reveal the Father and redeem humanity. To know Him is to know life itself.

So where do you go from here?

- Keep seeking God with your whole heart.
- Let Scripture shape your thinking and living.
- Bring your questions to God in prayer.
- Stay rooted in a community of faith.
- And trust that even when all your questions aren't answered, the One who holds the answers holds you too.

The Christian life is not primarily about information—it's about transformation. It's not just about what we believe, but who we are becoming. As the Apostle Paul wrote, "We all...are being transformed into His image with ever-increasing glory" (2 Corinthians 3:18, NIV).

May this book be a catalyst for that transformation in your life. And you may walk forward with confidence, not because you know everything, but because you know the One who does.

With wisdom, courage, and grace, keep going. God is with you.